Teacher Teams
That Get RESULTS

Gayle Gregory and Lin Kuzmich wish to dedicate this book to their loving families and future recipients of teacher knowledge and skill, their grandchildren. Without the support and inspiration of families and dedicated educators this work would not be possible.

Gayle H. Gregory | Lin Kuzmich

Teacher Teams
That Get **RESULTS**

61 Strategies for Sustaining and Renewing Professional Learning Communities

CORWIN PRESS
A SAGE Publications Company
Thousand Oaks, CA 91320

For information:

Corwin Press
A Sage Publications Company
2455 Teller Road
Thousand Oaks, California 91320
www.corwinpress.com

Sage Publications Ltd.
1 Oliver's Yard
55 City Road
London EC1Y 1SP
United Kingdom

Sage Publications India Pvt. Ltd.
B-42, Panchsheel Enclave
Post Box 4109
New Delhi 110 017 India

Printed in the United States of America

Library of Congress Cataloging-in-Publication Data

Gregory, Gayle.
Teacher teams that get results : 61 strategies for sustaining and renewing professional learning communities/Gayle H. Gregory, Lin Kuzmich.
    p. cm.
Includes bibliographical references and index.
ISBN-13: 978-1-4129-2612-6 (cloth : alk. paper)
ISBN-13: 978-1-4129-2613-3 (pbk. : alk. paper)
  1. Teaching teams. 2. Learning, Psychology of. I. Kuzmich, Lin. II. Title.
LB1029.T4G74 2007
371.14'8—dc22   2006028222

This book is printed on acid-free paper.

07 08 09 10 10 9 8 7 6 5 4 3 2

Acquisitions Editor:	Faye Zucker
Editorial Assistant:	Gem Rabanera
Production Editor:	Libby Larson
Copy Editor:	Julie Gwin
Typesetter:	C&M Digitals (P) Ltd.
Proofreader:	Theresa Kay
Indexer:	Michael Ferreira
Cover Designer:	Scott Van Atta
Graphic Designer:	Lisa Riley

Contents

Acknowledgments

Gayle Gregory and Lin Kuzmich wish to thank National Staff Development Council for the great work they do supporting educators and adult learning. In addition, we wish to thank Bobbie Johnson, a retired educator from Loveland, Colorado, for her outstanding help in reviewing and editing this publication. We also wish to thank the Corwin Press, Inc. staff for their continued assistance and support of our publications. We continue to learn from great staff development and teaming professionals whose contributions are referred to in this publication. Sharing and teaming in education is what this publication is all about and many fine authors and practitioners have contributed to the field of adult learning.

Gayle and Lin work with dedicated teachers and leaders who are working hard to meet the needs of diverse learners. This book is designed to help them continue to find their voice as they work together toward the growth and achievement of every student. Educators today face many challenges and they are our heroes. We hope this book helps them team together to accomplish great things for our students.

Corwin Press thanks the following reviewers for their contributions to this book:

Deborah Childs-Bowen, President
National Staff Development Council, GA

Terry Crawley, Coordinator for School Planning and Professional Development
Archdiocese of Louisville, Louisville, KY

Christelle Estrada, Director of Professional Development Services
Salt Lake City School District, Salt Lake City, UT

William Osman, President
New Jersey Staff Development Council, Hamilton Square, NJ

William Sommers, Teacher
Eden Prairie Public Schools, Eden Prairie, MN

Marion Woods, Coordinator of Professional Development
Little Rock School District, Little Rock, AR

About the Authors

 **Gayle H. Gregory** is a consultant, adjunct professor, and author from Burlington, Ontario, in Canada. She has been a teacher in elementary, middle, and secondary schools. She taught in schools with extended periods of instructional time (block schedules). She has had extensive districtwide experience as a curriculum consultant and staff development coordinator. Most recently, she was course director at York University for the Faculty of Education, teaching in the teacher education program. She now consults internationally (Europe, Asia, North and South America, Australia) with teachers, administrators, and staff developers in the areas of managing change, differentiated instruction, brain-compatible learning, block scheduling, emotional intelligence, instructional and assessment practices, cooperative group learning, presentation skills, renewal of secondary schools, enhancing teacher quality, coaching and mentoring, and facilitating large-scale change.

Gayle is affiliated with many organizations, including the Association for Supervision and Curriculum Development and the National Staff Development Council. Gayle is committed to lifelong learning and professional growth for herself and others. She may be contacted by phone at 905-336-6565 or e-mail at gregorygayle@netscape.net. Her Web site is www3.sympatico.ca/gayle.gregory.

 **Lin Kuzmich** is a consultant, adjunct professor, and author from Loveland, Colorado. She served Thompson School District as the assistant superintendent, executive director of secondary and elementary instruction, director of professional development, assistant director of special education, and as the building principal for nine years. Lin's school was named a 2000 winner of the John R. Irwin Award for Academic Excellence and Improvement. Lin has taught elementary, middle, and high school levels in both regular and special education. Lin earned the Teacher of the Year Award for Denver Public Schools in 1979 and was Northern Colorado Principal of the Year in 2000.

Lin is an adjunct professor at Colorado State University and University of Northern Colorado and also provides training for the Tointon Institute for Educational Change. She is a senior consultant for the International Center for Leadership in Education. Lin provides training and consulting to teachers and administrators around the country who wish to improve learning for all students, and she presents at numerous national conferences. Lin can be reached at 970-669-2290 or kuzenergy@gmail.com.

Gayle Gregory's National Publications

- *Designing Brain-Compatible Learning*
- *Thinking Inside the Block Schedule: Strategies for Teaching in Extended Periods of Time*
- *Differentiated Instructional Strategies: One Size Doesn't Fit All*
- *Differentiated Instructional Strategies in Practice: Training, Implementation, and Supervision*
- *Differentiation With Style to Maximize Student Achievement*
- Videos: Gayle is featured in the Video Journal of Educator's bestselling elementary and secondary videos, *Differentiating Instruction to Meet the Needs of All Learners.*

Lin Kuzmich's Government Publications

- *School Improvement Planning*
- *Data Driven Instruction Kit* and video
- *Facilitating Evaluation in a Standards-Based Classroom*

Gayle and Lin's Joint National Publications

- *Data Driven Differentiation in the Standards-Based Classroom*
- *Differentiated Literacy Strategies for Student Growth Grades K–6*
- *Differentiated Literacy Strategies for Student Growth Grades 7–12*
- Videos: Gayle and Lin are featured in the Video Journal of Education's recent elementary and secondary video: *Applied Differentiation: Making It Work in the Classroom*

Introduction

Tools That Get Results

Four years of public school teaching and ten years as a principal—convinces me the nature of relationships among adults who inhabit a school has more to do with a school's quality and character, with the accomplishments of its pupils and the professionalism of its teachers than any other factor.

—Roland Barth (2001, p. 105)

PURPOSE FOR THIS BOOK

For years, staff development was something we gave or did to teachers instead of actively engaging them. We did not get the sustained results or behavior changes that really affect student learning. As well, we failed to satisfy adult learning principles and what we know about how the brain operates. We know these things are best for learning with our students. Why won't we model them with educators so that they too learn optimally?

Dialogue matters. Teachers who have the opportunity to reflect and perfect their practices get better student results. Teachers often say they need more time to talk with colleagues, but fewer than half (46%) say that their overall professional development often or very often promotes collaboration. Teachers (36%) report that their staff development often recognizes and builds on their knowledge and experience. Only 26% of California teachers report that their professional development is often sustained over time, with ample participant follow-up and teacher support (Shields et al., 1999). Teachers and administrators who develop teams that support their learning needs as professionals find the stresses of change and accountability easier to manage. We tend to accomplish what we commit to, what we are clear about, what we value, and what we create. Therefore, the more we engage teachers in creating and deciding on actions, the more commitment they have to improve student growth. Thus, we are seeing results from teams who have taken on the ownership and leadership in our buildings. We can't mandate what matters. Teachers must own the changes. Thus it is essential that we come together to focus our attention on student learning. Whether we call it collaboration, teacher teams, or professional learning communities, the importance is the quest for student success in our schools. Throughout this book, we use the terms synonymously.

WHAT WE KNOW ABOUT ADULT LEARNING

Professional learning teams should tap into the brain's five natural learning systems (Given, 2002).

Social Learning System

"All of us prefer to interact with those whose presence increases the brain's feel-good neurotransmitter brain levels, resulting from feelings of comfort, trust, respect, and affection" (Panksepp, 1998). A system in place at birth relates to paired relationships. The other system progresses toward group relationships (Harris, 1998). It is a human basic need to feel that we belong and are accepted and included. The feelings of comfort, trust, respect, and affection increase the brain's feel-good neurotransmitter brain levels (Panksepp, 1998). As a member of a team that influences our natural tendencies and responses, we create more fertile conditions for our own learning and risk taking. Michael Fullan (2002) suggests that information only becomes knowledge through dialogue and meaning making. The use of cooperative group learning is essential in a classroom not only to allow the social system to flourish but also to help students achieve academic goals as well as social skills. It would provide the same for adults. Also, modeling and engaging in cooperative group learning will help teachers design successful group work in the classroom.

Emotional Learning System

People need to feel safe and supported to take risks. Adults also need challenging tasks with a minimal level of threat or risk to learn new skills. Emotions have a huge effect on the ability to focus and learn. It is endorphins and norepinephrine (the feel-good neurotransmitters released in the brain during positive experiences) that contribute to learning as well as good health (Pert, 1993).

The emotional system is embellished in schools

- Where educators and students believe all students will learn
- Where teacher differences are honored
- Where teachers connect the learning to students' lives
- Where teachers provide multiple ways for students to show what they know
- Where teachers continue to challenge students appropriately at their level
- Where the climate is supportive, inclusive, and predictable
- Where students and teachers celebrate the gains toward targeted standards
- Where students and teacher can laugh and celebrate together
- Where intrinsic motivation and pride in a job well done is fostered
- Where teachers celebrate incremental gains toward purposeful goals
- Where teachers' intrinsic motivation is fostered through goal setting and reflection

Physical Learning System

Active problem solving supports our physical needs. Interaction, movement, and creation of products are ways to develop a problem-solving orientation to learning. The physical system also demands movement to lower stress (adrenalin and cortisol, stress hormones in the bloodstream) and supply more oxygen and glucose to the brain. Adults feel purposeful when they are empowered to find or create solutions to problems and situations that matter to them. Physically being involved in learning new skills and practicing them taps into the physical learning system. Being actively involved in new experiences and models of teaching, assessment increases retention of the processes and greater increases the understanding and transfer into the classroom setting.

Cognitive Learning System

Conscious language development and focused attention increase memory. People need to use all senses to process new information. Facilitating learning by providing information in a novel way that stimulates all senses including the visual, auditory, and tactile senses, as well as taste and smell if appropriate, is what good teachers do. No less is necessary for adults. The emotional, social, and physical systems seem more greedy for attention, and if their needs are not met, people will not be able to focus on the learning, thus the cognitive system cannot work optimally. If all system needs are met, people tend to be more attentive and engaged in the learning process and ultimately are more successful in their learning. Allowing adults to read, view, process, and dialogue about new knowledge and skills creates multiple conditions for diverse learners to continue learning.

Reflective Learning System

This intelligence includes "thinking strategies, positive attitudes toward investing oneself in good thinking, and metacognition—awareness and management of one's own mind" (Perkins, 1995, p. 234). Damasio (1999) notes that the reflective system involves the interdependence of memory systems, communication systems, reason, attention, emotion, social awareness, physical experiences, and sensory modalities.

Metacognition, questioning, analysis, reaction, and goal setting all help us reflect on what we do and the results we get. It has been said that we learn from experience only if we reflect on the experience. We will not be able to sustain new learning without this type of reflective practice and dialogue. Teachers are making in excess of 2,500 decisions a day and need to reflect on what went well, should be changed, and done differently next time. We hone our craft and improve learning for students through considering our practice and making the changes necessary.

The reflective system allows us to

- Revisit and analyze situations
- Explore and react
- Create plans
- Facilitate progress toward goals

Teams who tap into all five "theaters of the mind" engage more diverse learners and increase the active processing of new information and skills in a variety of ways, thus increasing the chances of improving practice and behavior.

BRAIN BITS

If we advocate brain-compatible learning for students and then do not model the same strategies with adults, we send conflicting messages. Over the past 20 years, the emerging research and findings on how the brain operates have caused us to rethink student and adult learning (Buzan, 1991).

Certain factors help us meet and support the brain-based learning needs of people:

1. People need to feel safe: If we are asking people to risk, they need to do so in trustworthy environments. Building community is important.

2. People need to learn in a state of relaxed alertness: As with students, adults need high expectations with adequate support, encouragement, and feedback in a trusting environment.

3. People need learning that allows an emotional effect: Adults need a personal connection, need to satisfy an urge "to know," and need to know that their learning makes a difference for students.

4. People need social relationships: Adults crave validation and acceptance from colleagues. Collaboration creates the "pressure and support" needed for change to happen.

5. People need to form patterns, seek meaning and relevance, and set goals: Adults need to connect prior knowledge and experience to new ideas and to integrate the new learning with the old.

6. People enjoy an active learning environment that is engaging: Adults as students need to construct their own meaning from new knowledge and skill in a form that makes sense to an adult learner.

7. People need learning that supports multiple pathways to memory: Adults need variety and multisensory approaches to meet individual processing and learning needs. (adapted from Gregory & Parry, 2006)

ADULT LEARNING PRINCIPLES

Adult learning principles help us plan for the type of professional dialogue and interaction that supports learners who have years of life experiences to draw on. Adult learning principles interact with recent brain research. Our students have a variety of learning experiences that they bring to our classrooms. Adults are not different and the following four principles support all learners whose experiences shape how they create meaning and relevance and adapt their reasoning to both known and unknown circumstances.

Experiential:	**Self-Directed:**
Adults need to connect new ideas or actions to what they know and do well.	Adults need choice and opportunities to prioritize the work.
Life Applicable:	**Performance Centered:**
Adults need learning that has real life use and is transferable to their unique circumstances.	Adults like learning that is hands on, engaging, or gives them an opportunity for reflection.

Adapted from: Research from the study of adult learning (Barker, 1992; Bridges, 1991; Brookfield, 1988; Dalellew & Martinez, 1998; Knowles, 1980).

LEARNING STYLES

It has been said that education is a people business, a business about the diversity of people (Guild & Garger, 1985).

We face the issue of diversity in collaboration considering the various personalities or learning styles that are evident within the group.

For many years, experts have developed and shared a variety of theories that explain and identify people's learning styles. Learning styles indicate preferences those learners have in relation to how they acquire, process, and learn new information and skills.

We have used four analogies for the four learning styles that theorists and psychologists have identified. The objects not only typify the characteristics and preferences of the style but also are a helpful tool in remembering the four preferences. The following matrix shows the relationship between and among the different theories.

	Gregorc (1982)	*Kolb (1984)*	*True Colors (Lowry, 1979)*	*4MAT (McCarthy, 2000)*	*Silver/Strong/ Hanson (Silver & Hanson, 1998)*
Puppy	**Abstract Random** • Imaginative • Emotional • Holistic	**Diverger** Values positive, caring environments that are attractive, comfortable, and safe	**Blue** Best in open, interactive environments where teachers add a personal touch	**Type 1** Feel and reflect Create and reflect on experience	**Interpersonal** Appreciates concrete ideas and social interaction to process and use knowledge **SF (Sensing-Feeling)**
Microscope	**Abstract Sequential** • Intellectual • Analytical • Theoretical	**Assimilator** Avid reader who seeks to learn Patience for research Value concepts	**Green** Best when exposed to overall theory and interpretation	**Type 2 Analytical** Reflect and think Observers who appreciate lecture	**Understanding** Prefers to explore ideas and use reason and logic based on evidence **NT (Intuitive-Thinking)**
Clipboard	**Concrete Sequential** • Task oriented • Efficient • Detailed	**Converger** Values what is useful and relevant Immediacy and organizing the essential is important	**Gold** Best in well structured and clearly defined situations	**Type 3 Common Sense** Think and do Active, practical Make things work	**Mastery** Absorbs information concretely and processes step by step **ST (Sensing-Thinking)**
Beach ball	**Concrete Random** • Divergent • Experiential • Inventive	**Accommodator** Likes to try new ideas Values creativity, flexibility and opportunities	**Orange** Best in competitive situations especially with action	**Type 4 Dynamic** Creating and acting Usefulness and application of learning	**Self-Expressive** Uses feelings to construct new ideas Produces original or unique materials **NF (Intuitive-Feeling)**

What Different Learners Need

Beach balls. Beach balls respond to choice and options for experimentation and creativity. But we also must recognize that these learners need deadlines, guidelines, and boundaries or else they may have trouble focusing or completing assignments. Balancing their creativity and spontaneity with time management and "stick to it" skills can be very important for beach balls.

Clipboards. Clipboards like to have order, structure, and routine with clear guidelines and expectations. But life is not always predictable and organized. The unexpected occurs, and then what? Clipboards need to break out of the routine and learn to deal with ambiguity, spontaneity, and anomalies. Dealing with the unexpected is also a life skill.

Microscopes. Microscopes are more in-depth learners who like to analyze and investigate the truth they seek. They need sufficient time to go as deeply as they need for their learning, also recognizing that sometimes they have to move on. They also need help in working with others, developing collaborative skills, and seeing other people's point of view.

Puppies. Puppies are generally collaborative learners and enjoy partner and group work, yet they also need to develop independent skills and to take risks and learn to trust their own judgment and work alone in new areas.

Diversity, rather than being a problem in collaboration, is really a gift as we recognize the different strengths of various group members and capitalize on them. The awareness of styles and diversity in the group also helps each member to be cognizant and tolerant of the individuals and their contributions and limitations to the group process.

INITIAL GROUP DEVELOPMENT

Tuckman (1965) says that groups go through an evolution as they move toward collaboration and productivity as a team. It doesn't happen overnight or without skillful facilitation. The evolution is unique to each team based on its composition, intentions, as well as conscious will and skill. The time spent at each phase is individual, and the process is recursive. Emotions and determination will vary as teams become frustrated or feel incompetent over time. However, working consciously at each phase of the evolution will help move the team to a higher functioning, efficient group.

TEAM ADVANCEMENT WHEEL

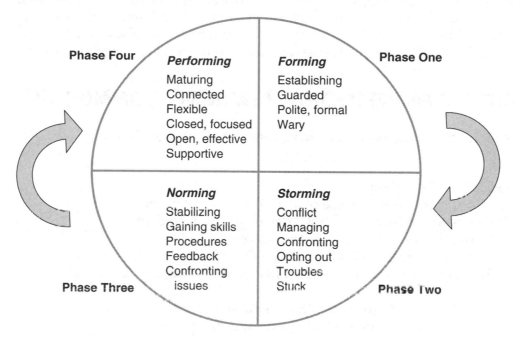

Relating Turnball to Strategies

Once we determine the phase a newly formed or existing group is at, we can select the strategies that help us move the group forward to the next stage. At each stage of the wheel, there are things the team members and leaders can do to help the evolution process in a positive way with less frustration and less time lost (Arbuckle & Murray, 1989).

PHASES OF GROUP DEVELOPMENT AND BEHAVIORS

Establishing: Forming Strategies to use: Building Climate and Sharing Knowledge	Members may be very positive or very apprehensive as the group begins to work together. They need to feel connected and included. This is done through team building activities and ice breakers. Members need opportunities get to know one another and build trust and relationships.
Dissatisfaction: Storming Strategies to use: Building Climate, Problem Solving, and Determining Priorities	It is during this time that members become more frustrated because of the need for clarification, purpose, and roles. People need strategies for conflict resolution and methods of making decisions and solving problems. This is also the conscious process of discussing openly what the team needs to succeed and sometimes redefining the tasks.
Stabilizing: Norming Strategies to use: Determining Priorities, Creating Excellence, and Building Resilience	Clarity helps the team move forward. Skill development helps members feel more competent and efficacious. Personal satisfaction increases, and team feels like it is beginning to jell.
Production: Performing Strategies to use: Sharing Knowledge and Skills, Creating Excellence, and Sustaining Change	The team is working well together and demonstrates creativity and resilience. There is autonomy and interdependence. Leadership is shared, and the best of each individual is used by the team to help more students succeed.

The buzz around professional learning communities has been loud and strong. However, without the right processing, we frustrate and discourage the growth of our staff and the ability to sustain change. Thus, it is our intent to provide a framework to understand the aspects of working together for student success, as well as processes to help adult learning teams succeed. We will help you tie the selection of process strategies to your desired results.

BENEFIT OF PROFESSIONAL LEARNING COMMUNITIES

Benefits for teachers who participate in high-quality professional learning teams include the following:

- Reduction of isolation
- Increased commitment to the school's mission and vision
- Shared responsibility for the total development of students
- Collective responsibility for student success
- Increased meaning and understanding of content
- Higher likelihood that teachers will be well informed, professionally renewed, and inspired
- More satisfaction, higher morale, lower absenteeism
- Significant advances in modifying teaching strategies
- Commitment to making significant and lasting changes.

The same research indicates results in the following specific benefits for students, if their teachers dialogue and interact with peers:

- Decreased dropout rate and fewer missed classes
- Lower rates of absenteeism
- Increased learning
- Greater gains in math, science, history, and reading
- Smaller achievement gaps between students from different backgrounds

Getting the maximum benefits from commitment, involvement, strong initiative, good inquiry, open advocacy, effective conflict resolution, solid decision making and extensive use of critique is what spectacular teamwork is all about.

—Blake, Mouton, and Allen (1987)

GETTING THE INTENDED RESULTS

The following model is our attempt to provide the organizational structure that illustrates the elements necessary to nurture and sustain your learning teams to accomplish results for students.

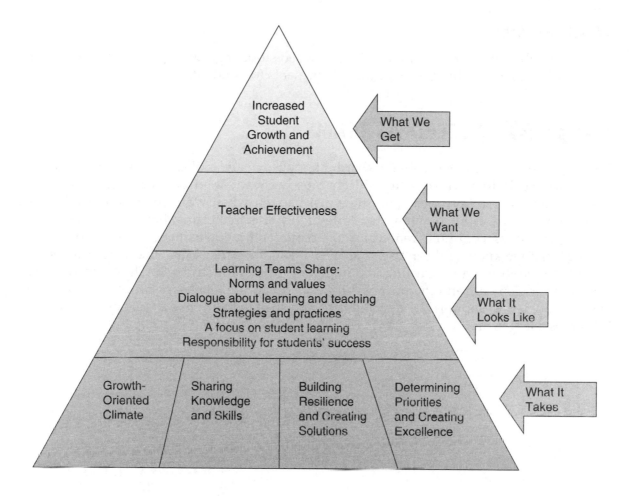

LEARNING TEAMS THAT GET RESULTS

What It Takes

Creating a growth-oriented climate, sharing knowledge and skills, building resilience, and determining priorities are essential to learning teams that get results. These four elements are foundational to provide the structure and purpose for teams to succeed. Without skills and processes to adequately nurture growth in these four areas, teams will flounder and participants will become frustrated. Frustrated teams abandon the work.

What It Looks Like

Successful learning teams share norms and values, continue to dialogue about teaching and learning, deprivatize strategies and practices, sustain a focus on student learning, and feel responsible for the success of all students.

What We Want

Ultimately, we want an effective teacher in every classroom who can reach and teach our diverse student population. We also need effective leaders at all levels; both administration and teacher leaders are necessary to foster and sustain change.

What We Get

Our collaborative efforts will result in increased student growth and achievement. What an incredible model of lifelong learning this presents for students.

TOOLS TO SUCCEED AS TEAMS

Creating a growth-oriented climate, sharing knowledge and skills, building resilience, and determining priorities is no easy feat. Just because we want or hear about professional learning communities doesn't mean that they just happen when we meet. There needs to be deliberate and conscious planning to create highly effective teams that sustain themselves in the process of continual renewal and accountability. Sustaining learning over time requires that we know and can use strategies in job-embedded ways that help groups continue to move forward in learning and in getting results for students. The following chart lists the four elements and the purposes for each. In addition, a list of processes and strategies is provided to support the development and sustainability of each element of successful professional teams.

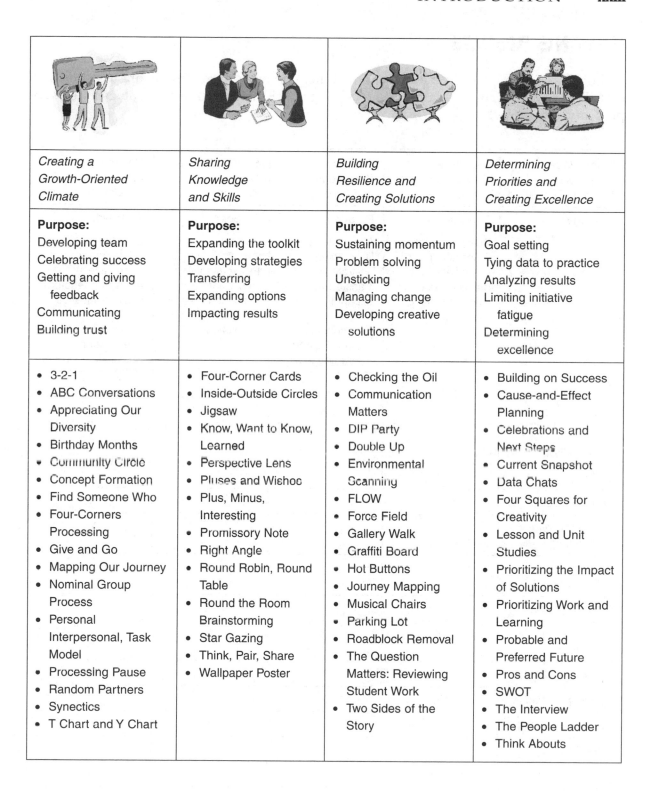

Creating a Growth-Oriented Climate	Sharing Knowledge and Skills	Building Resilience and Creating Solutions	Determining Priorities and Creating Excellence
Purpose: Developing team Celebrating success Getting and giving feedback Communicating Building trust	**Purpose:** Expanding the toolkit Developing strategies Transferring Expanding options Impacting results	**Purpose:** Sustaining momentum Problem solving Unsticking Managing change Developing creative solutions	**Purpose:** Goal setting Tying data to practice Analyzing results Limiting initiative fatigue Determining excellence
• 3-2-1 • ABC Conversations • Appreciating Our Diversity • Birthday Months • Community Circle • Concept Formation • Find Someone Who • Four-Corners Processing • Give and Go • Mapping Our Journey • Nominal Group Process • Personal Interpersonal, Task Model • Processing Pause • Random Partners • Synectics • T Chart and Y Chart	• Four-Corner Cards • Inside-Outside Circles • Jigsaw • Know, Want to Know, Learned • Perspective Lens • Pluses and Wishes • Plus, Minus, Interesting • Promissory Note • Right Angle • Round Robin, Round Table • Round the Room Brainstorming • Star Gazing • Think, Pair, Share • Wallpaper Poster	• Checking the Oil • Communication Matters • DIP Party • Double Up • Environmental Scanning • FLOW • Force Field • Gallery Walk • Graffiti Board • Hot Buttons • Journey Mapping • Musical Chairs • Parking Lot • Roadblock Removal • The Question Matters: Reviewing Student Work • Two Sides of the Story	• Building on Success • Cause-and-Effect Planning • Celebrations and Next Steps • Current Snapshot • Data Chats • Four Squares for Creativity • Lesson and Unit Studies • Prioritizing the Impact of Solutions • Prioritizing Work and Learning • Probable and Preferred Future • Pros and Cons • SWOT • The Interview • The People Ladder • Think Abouts

NOTE: SWOT = Strengths, weaknesses, opportunities, threats.

GETTING RESULTS

Although we have placed each process or strategy in one column, many are useful in several elements of successful teams. The following matrix helps you select strategies that support multiple purposes.

Elements of Successful Learning Teams	Creating a Growth-Oriented Climate	Sharing Knowledge and Skills	Building Resilience and Creating Solutions	Determining Priorities and Creating Excellence
Strategy	**Purpose:** Developing team Celebrating success Building trust Communicating Getting and giving feedback	**Purpose:** Affecting results Developing strategies Transferring Expanding options Expanding the teaching and learning toolkit	**Purpose:** Sustaining momentum Problem solving Unsticking Managing change Develop creative solutions	**Purpose:** Goal setting Tying data to practice Analyzing results Limiting initiative fatigue Celebrating excellence Sustaining results
3-2-1	X	X		
ABC Conversations	X	X		
Appreciating Our Diversity	X	X		
Birthday Months	X			
Building on Success		X	X	X
Cause-and-Effect Planning			X	X
Celebrations and Next Steps		X	X	X
Checking the Oil			X	X
Communication Matters	X	X	X	X
Community Circle	X	X		
Concept Formation	X	X	X	X
Current Snapshot			X	X
Data Chats		X	X	X
DIP Party			X	
Double Up		X	X	X
Environmental Scanning	X		X	X
Find Someone Who	X	X		

Elements of Successful Learning Teams	Creating a Growth-Oriented Climate	Sharing Knowledge and Skills	Building Resilience and Creating Solutions	Determining Priorities and Creating Excellence
FLOW			X	X
Force Field			X	X
Four-Corner Cards	X	X		
Four-Corners Processing	X	X		
Four Squares for Creativity		X	X	X
Gallery Walk		X	X	X
Give and Go	X	X		
Graffiti Board		X	X	
Hot Buttons			X	X
Inside-Outside Circles	X	X	X	
Jigsaw	X	X		
Journey Mapping		X	X	X
Know, Want to Know, Learned	X	X		X
Lesson and Unit Studies		X	X	X
Mapping Our Journey	X	X		
Musical Chairs		X	X	
Nominal Group Process	X		X	
Parking Lot			X	X
Personal, Interpersonal, Task Model	X	X		
Perspective Lens	X	X	X	
Plus, Minus, Interesting	X	X	X	
Pluses and Wishes	X	X		X
Prioritizing the Impact of Solutions			X	X

(Continued)

(Continued)

Elements of Successful Learning Teams	Creating a Growth-Oriented Climate	Sharing Knowledge and Skills	Building Resilience and Creating Solutions	Determining Priorities and Creating Excellence
Prioritizing Work and Learning			X	X
Probable and Preferred Future	X		X	X
Processing Pause	X	X		
Promissory Note	X	X	X	
Pros and Cons			X	X
Random Partners	X	X		
Right Angle	X	X	X	
Roadblock Removal	X		X	X
Round Robin, Round Table	X	X	X	
Round the Room Brainstorming	X	X	X	X
Star Gazing	X	X		
SWOT			X	X
Synectics	X	X		
T Chart and Y Chart	X	X		X
The Interview		X	X	X
The People Ladder		X	X	X
The Question Matters: Reviewing Student Work		X	X	X
Think Abouts		X	X	X
Think-Pair-Share	X	X		
Two Sides of the Story	X		X	
Wallpaper Poster	X	X		

NOTE: SWOT = Strengths, weaknesses, opportunities, threats.

IN THIS BOOK

The next four chapters explore each of the elements and thoroughly describe how to use these 61 processes and strategies to support your efforts. We use the terms *teams, professional learning communities*, and *learning groups* interchangeably in this book. Our primary focus is to provide strategies for adults who gather to learn, share, and get better at their craft so that students are successful academically and socially.

For each process or strategy, we included the following:

- The source for each strategy or process
- A purpose for the technique
- Basic information about the process, such as room arrangements, logistics, and what the process supports in the way of brain research and adult learning principles
- Directions for using the strategy
- When to use this method
- Examples and uses
- Where applicable, we include a template and model of a completed template or diagram

In the final chapter, we are going to provide you with suggested adult learning experiences and contexts that show you how to put these tools into practice. Each educator is busy trying to meet needs from every direction. We want to show you how to embed this type of practice into your busy schedule and maximize the results from the time you spend with other professionals.

Hopefully, this book will provide you with the appropriate tools you need to accomplish your goals and design successful adult learning and professional communities. The potential benefit to students if you succeed is enormous. We hope these tools help you sustain your successes and expand your potential to meet the needs of all students.

1

Creating a Growth-Oriented Culture

As a social resource for school improvement, relational trust facilitates the development of beliefs, values, organizational routines, and individual behaviors that instrumentally affect students' engagement and learning.

—Bryk and Schneider (2002, p. 115)

WHAT IS A GROWTH-ORIENTED CULTURE?

Culture is the intangible feeling that one gets when placed in an environment. It is the inclusive, exclusive, supportive, critical atmosphere that is created by those in the culture. Culture is often the major influence on why and how students learn and also on why and how teachers learn.

Teachers don't often create a different culture in their classrooms than is provided for them as adult learners. From our own experience, cultures that create conditions for learning are:

- Supportive
- Safe
- Inclusive
- Nonthreatening
- Free of blame and negativity
- Enabling
- Enthusiastic
- Trusting
- Open, so people can take risks without fear
- Sharing and problem solving
- Accepting of challenges

Culture speaks clearly but not always with words. Culture is conveyed through actions and subtleties. Cultures may be labeled as toxic, positive, negative, or enabling.

If a positive, enabling culture is not present, learners do not thrive. The climate at the school is not growth oriented. The classroom or the schoolhouse needs to be such that all people can learn and grow together, whatever their age. A growth-oriented climate results when these conditions exist.

The following chart suggests positive and negative indicators of climate.

Positive	Negative
Encouraging atmosphere	Toxic culture
Providing choices and variety	Unnecessary pressure
Providing appropriate time	Unrealistic time frames
Offering constructive feedback	Little or no feedback
Ensuring safety	Inappropriate challenges
Ensuring "relaxed alertness"	Uneasiness related to expectations
Offering helpful support and encouragement	Critical and judgmental environment
Honoring personality styles	Individual needs ignored

Deal and Peterson (1998) remind us that positive, successful cultures exhibit:

- A mission focused on student and teacher learning
- A rich sense of history and purpose
- Core values of collegiality, performance, and improvement that engender quality, achievement, and learning for everyone in the school
- Positive beliefs and assumptions related to students and to staff learning

- An informal network that fosters positive communication flows
- A strong professional community that uses knowledge, experience, and research to improve practice
- Leadership that balances continuity and improvement
- Rituals and ceremonies that reinforce core cultural values
- Stories that celebrate success and honor heroes and heroines
- An environment of joy and pride
- Respect and care for all

Trust

When we engage in group activities, comfort level comes from knowledge of one another and trust that grows over time. Trust develops through positive interaction fostered by formal and informal leadership.

EMOTIONAL INTELLIGENCE

Daniel Goleman (1995) suggests that there are five domains that constitute emotional intelligence:

- **Self-awareness of emotions:** Self-awareness is one's ability to sense and name a feeling when it happens and also to put it into words. Self-aware people can use appropriate strategies to deal with their moods by sharing frustrations with others or seeking support on a bad day.

- **Managing emotions:** Managing emotions is an outcome of recognizing and labeling feelings. It is the ability to calm and soothe during anxious moments or to manage and deal with anger.

- **Self-motivation:** Self-motivation consists of competencies such as persistence, setting one's own goals, and delaying gratification.

- **Empathy:** Empathy is being able to feel for another.

- **Social skills:** Social skills are the competencies that one uses to "read" other people and manage emotional interactions. People with high levels of social competencies have the ability to handle relationships well and are able to adapt to a variety of social situations.

WHY DO WE NEED A POSITIVE CLIMATE AND CULTURE?

The brain is on high alert for anything or anyone who might be a threat. A threat was formerly a snake or saber-tooth tiger when our ancestors lived on the savannah. Today it can be anything that is a perceived threat or a stressful experience. Many things are perceived threats to adult learners: the risk of failure, the fear of embarrassment, the lack of control, the sense of loss of efficacy, the feeling of being isolated and not part of a group.

The following six factors affect how people cope in stressful situations (Witmer, Rich, Barcikowski, & Mague, 1983):

1. If people have self-esteem and feelings of self-worth and efficacy, they are more able to adapt and cope with stress. If they feel that they belong and are accepted in the group or feel special or unique in some way, situations are less stressful and they feel more able to cope.

2. People need to have a sense of control over their lives and the freedom to monitor their lives and emotions based on their workable set of values and beliefs.

3. People need to have a sense of internal control over their life pace and their emotions.

4. Irrational beliefs have a lot to do with how people cope with change.
   a. Past experience with successful change and the development of new skills and procedures
   b. Approval for effort and success, positive feedback

5. Social support is essential: Professional learning communities provide support systems so that teachers can problem solve, plan, and dialogue about teaching and learning. They help teachers deprivatize their teaching and focus on the implementation of best practices so all students may succeed.

6. Job and life meaning: Adults generally, as self-directed learners, seek strategies to develop skills to be successful in their work. Contributing in a positive way and seeing relevance and meaning in their work is satisfying and energizing.

RISK FACTORS

Risk factors need to be considered when we ask adults to step out of their comfort zone. In professional learning communities, we want people to feel safe to risk changing their behavior and practices, to face failure and challenges with a "can do" attitude. Supportive energy will enable more learners to be successful. We, of course, need to start small and think big. People don't jump off the high-diving board until they have confidence to jump off the lower board in a well-supervised area (maybe even with water wings). Teachers are more apt to work with one other trusted colleague on their journey toward deprivatization of practice than share ideas with the whole faculty. Considering what level of risk is appropriate for adults is often a key to getting people to take a chance. People pushed beyond their safety level will not take or will hesitate to take action. People who see that the risk level is manageable are enabled to risk a change of behavior.

Andy Hargreaves and Ruth Dawe (1989) note that there are several types of cultures that exist in the schoolhouse: isolation, balkanization, contrived congeniality, and true collaboration. The following chart shows the four kinds of culture and behaviors that might be exhibited in each one.

Isolation/ Individualism *Lone Ranger*	Balkanization *Camps*	Contrived Congeniality *I Don't Need to Hold Hands*	True Collaboration *Let's Work Together*
• Individual planning • Private discipline	• Groups, clichés, or departments work together and exclude others • Often develop "group think" • More closed-minded over time	• Forced situations • Committees • Grade group teams • Focus groups	• Grade groups focused on student needs • Vertical teams developing scope and sequence or curriculum mapping • Lateral teams developing consistency • Selected groups focused on a particular issue • Inquiry or research

How Do We Do It?

Teams evolve through predictable phases. As mentioned previously, teams develop over time. The first stage is that of forming, where members wonder about purpose, operating procedures, power, and control in the group. We know that people need to feel connected, safe, and unself-conscious if they are going to be free to think, be creative, and risk suggesting and offering ideas.

PRIMARY PURPOSE FOR
THE STRATEGIES IN THIS SECTION

In this chapter, we offer you strategies to build a climate conducive to learning and growing, including the following:

- Developing a team
- Celebrating success
- Getting and giving
- Giving feedback
- Communicating
- Building trust

ABC Conversations

Purpose: Creating a Growth-Oriented Climate

This strategy gives people a chance to listen intently to one person at a time and offers a captive audience. It allows for a sharing of ideas or problem solving.

It makes a good processing tool at the end of a session so that individuals can share their intentions and concerns about an idea or topic.

Basics

Number of Participants	May be done in small table groups of three or in an "eye to eye, knee to knee" chair cluster
Time Needed	15–20 minutes
Room Arrangement	Table groups, chair clusters, or standing
Difficulty Level	Low risk, moderately easy
Brain Bits	Emotional impact and social support, development of cognitive learning in terms of developing common vocabulary, clarifying, and sharing
Brain's Natural Learning Systems	Social, cognitive, physical, reflective
Adult Learning Principle	Experiential: connects to what we know and do well
	Life application: determines real-life use and process of transfer to participants' unique circumstances
Materials	Scribe recording sheet

Process Directions

1. Form triads.

2. Each person takes a letter: A, B, C.

3. Person A is the Questioner, Person B is the Respondent, and Person C is the Scribe.

4. In the first round, each performs his or her role.

5. In the second round, each performs a new role (see figure).

6. In the third round, each performs a new role (see figure).

When

- Participants need some active involvement related to their own well-being.
- People need a change of state and another colleague to discuss an idea.
- People need to move or get up.
- The facilitator needs to lower the risk for participation.
- Dialogue and creating consensus are necessary.
- There is a need for team building.

Examples and Uses

1. Since our last meeting, what have you done to use a Venn diagram with your students?

    What content was used?

    What went well?

    What would you do differently next time you use a Venn with students?

2. Could be used for problem solving.

    What is most problematic when you ask students to work in groups?

    How have you handled this in the past?

    What help would you like?

3. What idea interested you most from this session?

    What strategy would you like to implement?

    What standard or expectation will you target?

    What content will you use?

    What adjustments will you make to help students be successful?

Selected References

Annenberg Institute for School Reform (1998); Buehl (2006); Chadwick (2006); Elder and Paul (2002); Lipton, Humbard, and Wellman (2001).

ABC Conversation

A Questioner
B Respondent
C Scribe

C Questioner
A Respondent
B Scribe

B Questioner
C Respondent
A Scribe

Round 1	Round 2	Round 3
A Questioner	B Questioner	C Questioner
B Respondent	C Respondent	A Respondent
C Scribe	A Scribe	B Scribe

Scribe Form

	Notes:	Reflections:
Person A_____		
Person B_____		
Person C_____		

STRATEGY 2

Birthday Months

Purpose: Creating a Growth-Oriented Climate

This strategy is good to get participants' voices in the room, even with larger groups, or note learning from start of session to the end of session. This is also great for creating a simple processing break.

Basics

Number of Participants	May be done in small table groups or as a large group
Time Needed	10–15 minutes
Room Arrangement	Table groups
Difficulty Level	Low risk, easy
Brain Bits	Emotional impact and social support, development of cognitive learning in terms of developing common vocabulary, clarifying, and sharing
Adult Learning Principle	Experiential: connects to what we know and do well Life application: determines real-life use and process of transfer to participants' unique circumstances
Materials	Chart paper and markers

Process Directions

1. Have participants group themselves by birthday months or seasons at various points in the room.

2. Give a prompt and ask participants to discuss with a partner within that grouping.

3. The facilitator asks for responses to prompt from partners, taking several examples.

When

- Participants need some active involvement related to their own well-being.
- People need a change of state and another colleague to discuss an idea.
- People need to move or get up.
- The facilitator needs to lower the risk for participation.
- Dialogue and creating consensus are necessary.
- There is a need for team building beyond table groupings.
- Groups are large and need to process.

Examples and Uses

1. Use at the beginning and end of day with the same prompt to support learning.

2. Use to introduce each other.

3. Use to get participants up and sharing points of view or experiences related to the training topic.

Selected References

Garmston (1996), Sousa (2004), Wellman and Lipton (2003).

ROOM ARRANGEMENTS

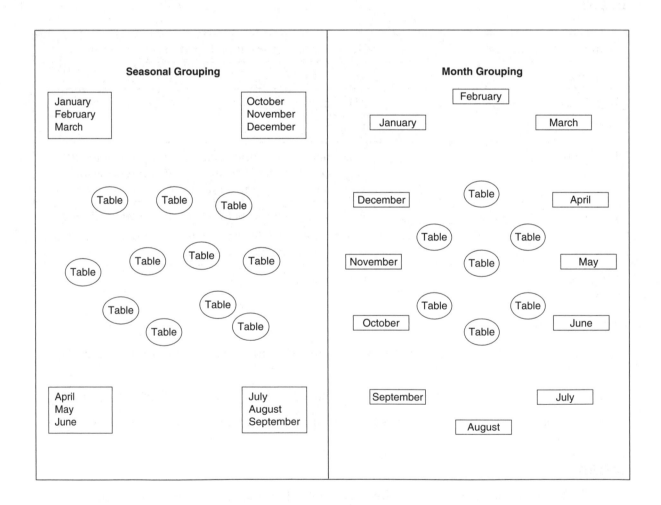

STRATEGY 3

Community Circle

Purpose: Creating a Growth-Oriented Climate

A safe, connected community circle allows participants to feel included and have a voice and creates a positive climate. It is a vehicle for sharing, reflecting, discussing, and celebrating.

Basics

Number of Participants	May be done in several small groups or as a large group
Time Needed	10–15 minutes
Room Arrangement	Chairs in a circle or sitting on carpet so everyone can see everyone else
Difficulty Level	Low risk, easy
Brain Bits	Emotional impact and social support, development of cognitive learning in terms of developing common vocabulary, clarifying, and sharing
Brain's Natural Learning Systems	Emotional, social, reflective, physical, cognitive
Adult Learning Principle	Experiential: connects to what we know and do well

Life application: determines real-life use and process of transfer to participants' unique circumstances |
| Materials | None |

Process Directions

Ask participants to bring chairs and sit in a circle where everyone can see everyone. (Chairs may be set up previously or a carpeted area could be used so participants sit on the floor.)

1. A prompt or question is posed, and people are given time to think of a response.

2. Ask for someone to volunteer to start.

3. Go around the circle—each person speaks in turn.

4. If someone is not ready to share or needs a little more think time, Right to Pass may be used. The person will say "Pass," and then the facilitator will move on to the next person. People who pass will be asked to respond later.

When

- You want people to share ideas that the whole group can see and hear.
- You want to celebrate things that have been accomplished.
- You want to discuss critical issues in close proximity with equal footing and position.

Examples and Uses

1. At the end of a meeting, each person in the circle may give a thank you to someone on the team for their contribution that day.

2. A use may be to share opinions about an issue. Each person, in turn, gives a perspective or point of view concerning the issue.

3. Each person shares how he or she feels about an issue or suggestion.

Selected References

Annenberg Institute for School Reform (1998), Australian Government Department of Education (DOE, 2006), Chadwick (2006), Gibbs (2001).

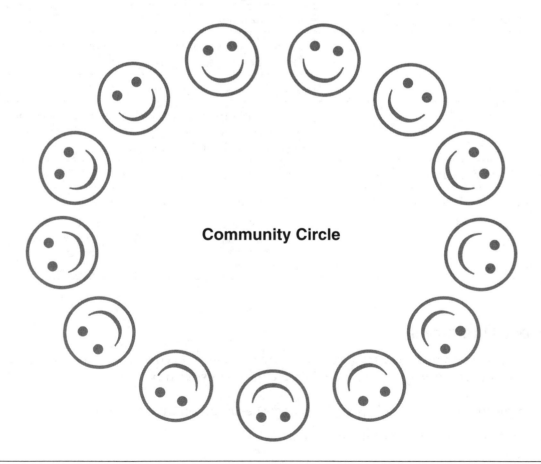

Community Circle

STRATEGY 4

Concept Formation

Purpose: Creating a Growth-Oriented Climate

When establishing working norms for team success, people often need to articulate what is important to them and clarify behaviors expected of all team members. Concept formation can be used as a way of getting consensus and organization from a brainstorm of ideas.

Basics

Number of Participants	May be done in small table groups or as a large group
Time Needed	15–20 minutes
Room Arrangement	Table groups
Difficulty Level	Low risk, easy
Brain Bits	Emotional impact and social support, development of cognitive learning in terms of developing common vocabulary, clarifying, and sharing
Brain's Natural Learning Systems	Social, physical, cognitive
Adult Learning Principle	Experiential: connects to what we know and do well Life application: determines real-life use and process of transfer to participants' unique circumstances
Materials	Self-sticking chart paper and markers

Process Directions

1. Suggest a topic so that participants have a focus for brainstorming a data set.

2. Give each participant in the group at least five to six self-sticking notes.

3. Have each person jot down one idea per note.

4. Have people share their notes in the center of the table, and begin organizing them in clusters based on like attributes.

5. Once participants are satisfied with the arrangement, have them label each cluster with a title that is representative of the grouping.

6. You might want to use the acronym GROUP to remember the steps in the process:
   - Generate data or gather them from another source
   - Re-examine

- Organize by similarities
- Use a label to identify groups
- Process and discuss

This is much more of a constructivist approach to concept attainment through participants' knowledge and personal input of generating data.

7. Sometimes participants may be given a data set and asked to organize it. They may not have the background to create data or data are already available, and it wastes time to go through the generation process.

When

- Participants need some active involvement related to their own well-being.
- Active involvement of personal ideas and a kinesthetic task is needed.
- Dialogue and creating consensus are necessary.
- There is a need for team building.

Examples and Uses

1. Use to generate and come to consensus on norms for the group to live by. Participants will generate behaviors that are important to them as the group works together over time. These can be clustered and discussed, and several norms or rules to live by can be identified.

2. Use to generate priorities for a team to work on. Each person generates three to five priorities, and then the team clusters and labels the groups. From this, the team can prioritize and move to planning such as a "People Ladder."

3. "What is quality teaching?" may be another prompt for which people can generate attributes.

4. "What assessment tools do you use?" may be another way to generate strategies and share ideas while dialoguing about teaching and learning.

Selected References

Beaudoin and Taylor (2004), Chang and Dalziel (1999a), Erickson (2005), Marzano (2004), Taba (1967), Wald and Castleberry (2000).

EXAMPLE: ASSESSMENT TOOLS I USED THIS WEEK

Ask each person in the group to generate (one per sticky note) which assessment tools he/she used this week.

Generated data set for one group of three:

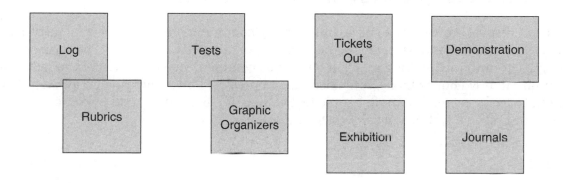

Clusters identified:

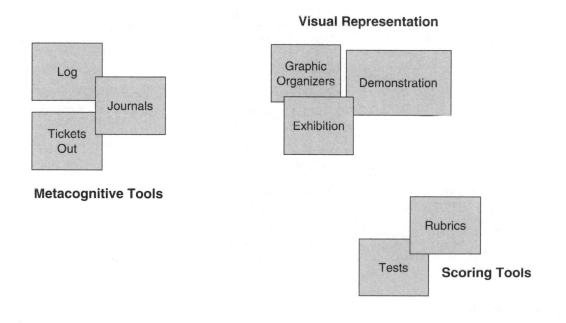

After considering strategies others used, what can I add to my repertoire to inform me about how my students are learning?

STRATEGY 5

Appreciating Diversity

Purpose: Creating a Growth-Oriented Climate

Trust and respect are key for a successful learning community to thrive. Each of us has a different background and different experiences. We also have different preferences and strengths in multiple intelligences that tend to be complementary as we work together. It is important that we honor those differences and appreciate how they bring greater depth and capability to the team. The more people feel valued, the more they tend to continue to contribute and receive feelings of self-worth and self-confidence.

Basics

Number of Participants	Anyone in the group may show appreciation at any time, but it may be something that the team wants to build in
Time Needed	Very little time is needed to show appreciation to others
Room Arrangement	Not applicable
Difficulty Level	Low
Brain Bits	Emotional impact and social support, development of cognitive learning in terms of developing common vocabulary, clarifying, and sharing One of the basic human needs is to belong and feel valued
Brain's Natural Learning Systems	Social, emotional, physical, cognitive
Adult Learning Principle	Sociability
Materials	Simple to none. Award cards

Process Directions

1. Participants could use a preference inventory to identify their dominant style.

2. The analogies on page xvii in the introduction could serve as a discussion piece and each team member could identify their own preferences.

3. Team members could then brainstorm what they feel would be valuable about each style and what each would bring to the group.

4. At the end of each session together, team members thank each other for the strengths that each has brought to the group.

When

- Participants need to appreciate the diversity within the team.
- Annoyance surfaces when others' styles get in the way of progress of the team.
- Team building needs to continue.

Examples and Uses

1. Use this protocol to include new members to a team.

2. Use this strategy to make certain all voices and viewpoints are heard and respected on a controversial new initiative.

3. Use this strategy when the team needs to move beyond storming and norming.

4. The following charts can be used to brainstorm qualities of each preference (see page xvii for characteristics of each of these styles).

Puppies	Microscopes

Clipboards	Beach Balls

5. At the end of a meeting each participant needs to express appreciation for contributions from others. Perhaps a round robin expression of thanks would suffice.

6. Teams can create awards for helpful behavior of team members. The Creativity Award, To The Rescue, Possibility Thinker, Action Oriented.

7. The Giving of Roses: Every week a rose can be given to a staff member who goes "beyond the call" for another member staff. Teachers or administration drop a name in the "Rose Bowl" suggesting a recipient each week. It has been said that people would appreciate one rose and an encouraging word from a friend rather than a room full when they are dead and can't appreciate them.

8. At the end of each meeting participants could discuss how their differences contributed to the success of the session.

Possibility Thinking...

This award is given to _____

For _____ to

_____

_____

Date: _____

Creativity Award

This award is given to _____

For helping us to _____

_____

Date: _____

To the Rescue

This award is given to _____

for helping _____ to

_____

_____

Date: _____

Action Oriented

This award is given to _____

For _____ to

_____

_____

Date: _____

Giving the Rose...

This award is given to _____

For _____ to

_____

_____

Date: _____

STRATEGY 6

Find Someone Who

Purpose: Creating a Growth-Oriented Climate

"Find Someone Who" or the "People Search" can be used as a getting-to-know-you activity or an ice breaker. It can be used with personal information or instructional material that people need to dialogue about.

Basics

Number of Participants	Any number works as long as they are able to move about in the space provided
Time Needed	10–15 minutes
Room Arrangement	Area where people can walk about and interact
Difficulty Level	Low risk, easy
Brain Bits	Emotional impact and social support, development of cognitive learning in terms of developing common vocabulary, clarifying, and sharing
Brain's Natural Learning Systems	Social, reflective, physical, cognitive
Adult Learning Principle	Experiential: connects to what we know and do well, uses people as valuable resources Life application: determines real-life use and process of transfer to participants' unique circumstances
Materials	Paper and pencil

Process Directions

1. Give participants a Bingo grid or list of items for which they need to find someone to answer or give them information.

2. Each person takes his or her list and walks around the room trying to find someone who is able to give an answer to a question on the sheet.

3. The person listens attentively to the answer that is given and jots down the name of the person who answered the question beside the question.

4. When everyone has completed his or her grid, people can report what they have heard and learned from others.

When

- Participants need some active involvement related to developing connections and relationships with others on the team.
- People need a change of state and another colleague to discuss an idea.
- People need to move or get up.
- The facilitator needs to lower the risk for participation.
- There is a need for team building.
- Content needs to be shared and discussed.

Examples and Uses

1. If the staff is implementing differentiated instruction, a People Search may yield statements that would foster dialogue and keep the implementation going.

2. This can be used for sharing of thoughts on a particular topic.

3. This can be used for sharing what works with a set of skills after teachers have had time to practice in their classrooms.

Selected References

Barell (2003); Bellanca and Fogarty (1994); Dunne, Nave, and Lewis (2000); Hill and Eckert (1995); Hill and Hill (1990); Reid (2002); Robertson and Kagan (1992); Silver, Strong, and Perini (1997).

Examples

FIND SOMEONE WHO:

1. Has created and can describe a challenging assignment for more able learners in his or her class

_____

2. Can explain why it is important to differentiate instruction in the classroom

_____

3. Can tell one way he or she establishes FLOW

_____

4. Can share his or her thoughts on compacting

_____

5. Can define cubing and explain how he or she uses it

_____

6. Can explain how to use Multiple Intelligences to differentiate

_____

7. Will share how to use focus and sponge activities in his or her classroom

_____

More Examples:

People Searches can also be done on a Bingo card.

FIND SOMEONE WHO CAN TELL YOU . . .

One way to help students be self-reliant	One way to manage homework	A suggestion to help motivate learners
A note-taking and summarizing skill	A way to promote metacognition	An assessment that gives immediate data
A strategy to challenge high-ability learners	A vocabulary technique that works	An answer to a question you have about differentiation

Blank Bingo Card to Create Your Own Processing Prompts

STRATEGY 7

Four-Corners Processing

Purpose: Creating a Growth-Oriented Climate

This is a great strategy for self-examination, reflection, and evaluation. People choose a corner where they think they belong based on experience, opinion, point of view, or response.

Basics

Number of Participants	Four corners of the room are labeled appropriately depending on the topic
Time Needed	10–15 minutes
Room Arrangement	Corners
Difficulty Level	Higher risk, easy to do
Brain Bits	Emotional impact and social support, development of cognitive learning in terms of developing common vocabulary, clarifying, and sharing
Brain's Natural Learning Systems	Physical, cognitive, reflective, social
Adult Learning Principle	Experiential: connects to what we know and do well Life application: determines real-life use and process of transfer to participants' unique circumstances
Materials	Signs for the corners of the room

Process Directions

1. Decide what signs you need in the corners. PowerPoint or overhead directions could be used as well (see the following).

2. Participants are given a prompt and a minute or two to think about their response.

3. Then people are asked to go to the corner of their choice and be ready to share their rationale for their decision to go there.

4. When people arrive in their corner, they meet up with someone else and share their rationale.

5. Each pair can meet another pair and continue the conversation.

When

- Participants need some active involvement related to their own well-being.
- People need a change of state and another colleague to discuss an idea.

- People need to move or get up.
- Dialogue and creating consensus are necessary.
- There is a need for team building and perspective taking.

Examples and Uses

1. Ask participants how they feel about adopting a block schedule.

2. Ask participants what they think differentiation is or is not.

Selected References

Gibbs (2001), Hill and Hill (1990), Reid (2002).

Examples of Four-Corner Templates

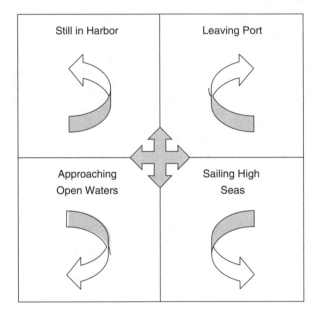

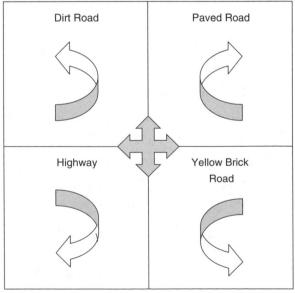

STRATEGY 8

Give and Go

Purpose: Creating a Growth-Oriented Climate

This strategy can be used when there is a need for generating ideas, sharing ideas, or giving the group an opportunity to transfer ideas learned in a session or discuss.

Basics

Number of Participants	Any number would work
Time Needed	5 minutes
Room Arrangement	Doesn't matter
Difficulty Level	Low risk, easy
Brain Bits	Emotional impact and social support, development of cognitive learning in terms of developing common vocabulary, clarifying, and sharing
Brain's Natural Learning Systems	Physical, cognitive, reflective
Adult Learning Principle	Experiential: connects to what we know and do well Life application: determines real-life use and process of transfer to participants' unique circumstances
Materials	Paper and pen or pencil

Process Directions

1. On your form, list two strategies you use for _____.

2. Meet with another person. Share one of your ideas. Record his or her idea on your form.

3. Continue meeting new colleagues until you have 10 new ideas.

When

- Participants need some active involvement related to their own well-being.
- People need a change of state and another colleague to discuss an idea.
- People need to move or get up.
- The facilitator needs to lower the risk for participation.
- Dialogue and creating consensus are necessary.
- There is a need for team building.
- The group wants to brainstorm.

Examples and Uses

You may ask people to:

1. List ways they collect student data.

2. List ways to help students review for a test.

3. List ways to increase student involvement.

4. List ways to have students dialogue.

Selected References

Dunne et al. (2000), Hill and Eckert (1995), Reid (2002), Silver et al. (1997).

Give and Go

1. _____

2. _____

3. _____

4. _____

5. _____

6. _____

7. _____

8. _____

9. _____

10. _____

Give and Go

1. _____

2. _____

3. _____

4. _____

5. _____

6. _____

7. _____

8. _____

9. _____

10. _____

STRATEGY 9

Mapping Our Journey

Purpose: Creating a Growth-Oriented Climate

Identifying where a group came from and where to go next is a great way to honor the work. This helps a group build initial trust that the hard work of the past will not be forgotten as it moves forward.

Basics

Number of Participants	May be done in small table groups or as a large group
Time Needed	20–30 minutes initially and ongoing
Room Arrangement	Table groups
Difficulty Level	Low risk, easy
Brain Bits	Emotional impact and social support, development of cognitive learning in terms of developing common vocabulary, clarifying, and sharing
Adult Learning Principle	Experiential: connects to what we know and do well Life application: determines real-life use and process of transfer to participants' unique circumstances
Materials	Chart paper and markers Bulletin board

Process Directions

The following is a guideline of the process, but you may begin by identifying the destination first or the catalyst first. This can also be a recursive process, as we never know when a setback may occur or an action may really click and propel us forward.

1. Create a bulletin board that will show the journey of the group or school in its improvement efforts.

2. The first step is to identify the current state. Where are we now?

3. The next is to articulate the future state in detail.

4. There may be a need to name the catalyst or impetus for the changes sought.

5. Then there is a backward mapping process to identify actions that need to be taken to continue the journey.

6. As in a process or journey, there may be roadblocks or pitfalls that may occur.

7. These setbacks may result in the need for rolling planning (the sense to monitor, assess, and adjust plans based on feedback and changes that occur). It is always smart to change plans and designs to respond to the challenges, new information, or "bumps in the road" that everyone faces in a change process. It doesn't make sense to continue on the wrong road when evidence or experience tells us differently. Visually posting and examining the issues will help the group progress in spite of setbacks.

8. Visuals also concretely represent progress and reason for celebration.

9. This allows people to step back and examine what works and what doesn't so that by reflecting on the process, we get better at problem solving and at planning in the future.

When

- Participants need some active involvement related to their own well-being.
- People need a change of state and another colleague to discuss an idea.
- People need to move or get up.
- The group needs an opportunity to create a visual representation of a journey.
- We are building initial trust and the work that went before us needs to be honored and remembered to continue into the future.

Examples and Uses

1. A group is trying to close the math gap more rapidly (see example).

2. Several new teachers have joined the group, and the group is trying to move forward by first reviewing where it is and what it has done so far.

3. Several members of the group are worried about potential problems as planning for the future proceeds. It is better to acknowledge and label the issues and then plan for these worries than it is to ignore concerns. This helps a group build team spirit and create a climate where hopes and fears are addressed respectfully.

Selected References

Bailey (1995), Chadwick (2006), Chang and Dalziel (1999b), Gregory and Kuzmich (2004), Roberts and Pruitt (2003), Wald and Castleberry (2000).

Mapping Our Journey

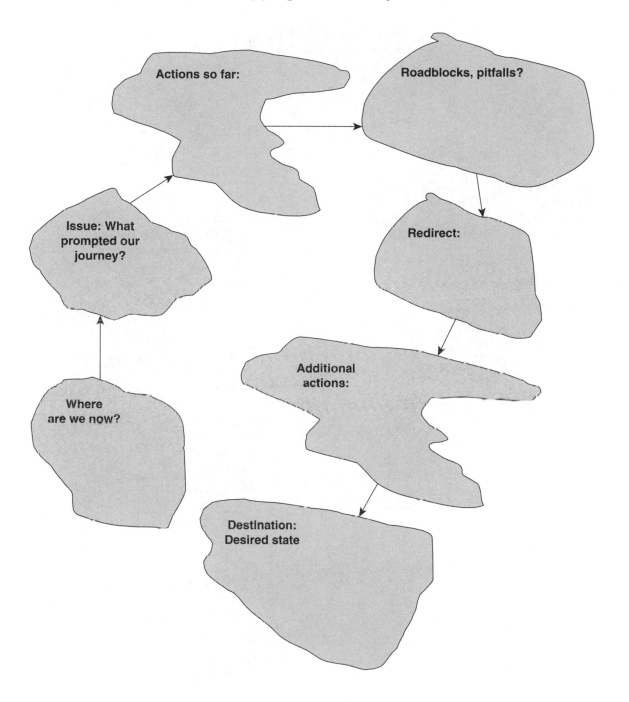

Actions so far:

Roadblocks, pitfalls?

Issue: What prompted our journey?

Redirect:

Where are we now?

Additional actions:

Destination: Desired state

Mapping Our Journey: An Example

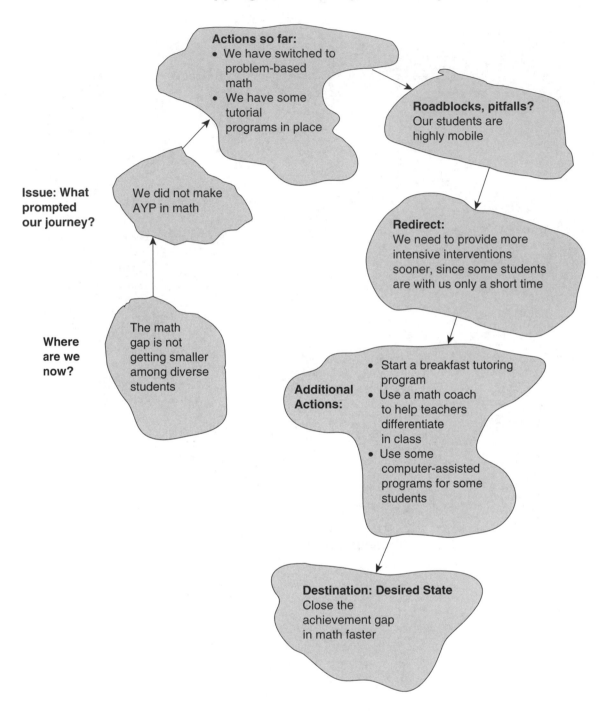

Actions so far:
- We have switched to problem-based math
- We have some tutorial programs in place

Roadblocks, pitfalls?
Our students are highly mobile

Issue: What prompted our journey?

We did not make AYP in math

Redirect:
We need to provide more intensive interventions sooner, since some students are with us only a short time

Where are we now?

The math gap is not getting smaller among diverse students

Additional Actions:
- Start a breakfast tutoring program
- Use a math coach to help teachers differentiate in class
- Use some computer-assisted programs for some students

Destination: Desired State
Close the achievement gap in math faster

STRATEGY 10

3-2-1

Purpose: Creating a Growth-Oriented Climate

When establishing working norms for team success, people often need to clarify what is important to them and clarify behaviors.

Basics

Number of Participants	May be done individually, in small table groups, or as a large group
Time Needed	5–6 minutes
Room Arrangement	N/A
Difficulty Level	Low risk, easy
Brain Bits	Emotional impact and social support, development of cognitive learning in terms of developing common vocabulary, clarifying, and sharing
Brain's Natural Learning Systems	Cognitive, reflective
Adult Learning Principle	Experiential: connects to what we know and do well Life application: determines real-life use and process of transfer to participants' unique circumstances
Materials	Chart paper and markers for large group Small pieces of paper or self-sticking notes for individual participants

Process Directions

1. Choose method of use:
   a. Distribute 3-2-1 cards to be filled in by participants as a ticket out at the end of a session.
   b. The 3-2-1 prompt can also be put on the whiteboard or overhead, and people can respond on a self-sticking note.
   c. Create a template and distribute it.

2. Ask participants to fill out their cards individually.

3. Process as a small or large group.

4. Use information to help focus the next steps of the group's work or as feedback for a meeting or session. Be certain to share the results, and have the facilitator describe how the group can use the results.

When

- Participants need some active involvement related to their own learning.
- Use to tap into relevance and meaning related to new learning.
- Use to evoke commitment through writing specific steps each person commits to for implementation.
- Use to give data to help fine tune next steps for a group.
- Use to give information about the group process and how well it is meeting needs.

Examples and Uses

1. At the end of a session, people need to reflect on their involvement, learning, and commitment or goals.

2. 3-2-1 can also be used at the beginning of a session to reconnect with the last time the group was together.

3. It is easy to collect data sources for monitoring group learning or process when working on specific topics, especially as a group is just learning new things.

4. The following examples give suggestions for prompts.

Selected References

Garmston (1996); Jones (1998); Zygouris-Coe, Wiggins, and Smith (2004).

3	Things you learned
2	Things that intrigued you
1	Thing you could share with others

3	Things you liked
2	Concerns you have
1	Thing you intend to do

3	Things that interest me
2	Things I would like to try
1	Thing I wonder about . . .

"What's on your mind?" is another reflective technique that can be used to close a team meeting. It gives people a chance to reflect and share their thinking with others. Here are three examples that you might use:

What's On Your Mind?

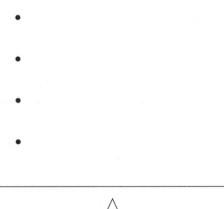 4 ideas that I remember from last session

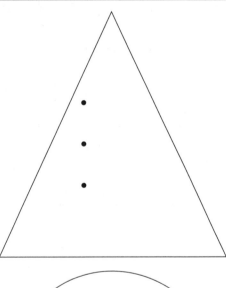 3 connections that I made for my work

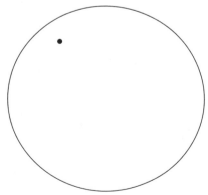 1 question that is still rolling around in my head

---

What's On Your Mind?

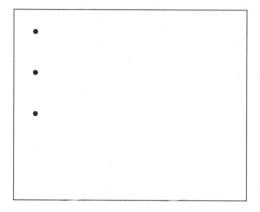

3 ideas that squared with my values and belief

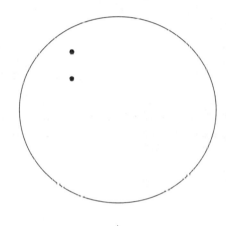

2 ideas rolling around in my head

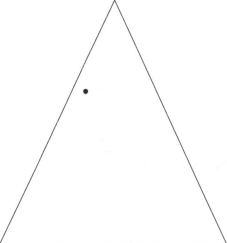

1 idea that piqued my curiosity

3-2-1 Warm-up

3	List three changes you noticed in staff dialogue or conversations in the last year or two: • • •
2	List two things you may hear (or see) that might tell you the learning networks in your building or department are shifting their conversations so that more students will be successful (use your book and handouts to help you): • •
1	List one question you have about leading your learning networks: •

STRATEGY 11

Nominal Group Process

Purpose: Creating a Growth-Oriented Climate

It is important for comfort and consistency to establish norms or standard working procedures for working together. This way people feel safe and comfortable about how they are going to be treated and will be more able to trust the process of their work together. If people are allowed to state what is important to them in working relationships and protocols and have that clarified at the onset, there is often less conflict throughout the team process, thus they move to quality work together sooner.

Basics

Number of Participants	This may be accomplished with any number of participants often working in small groups and coming to consensus by sharing the small-group norms that can be synthesized to form whole-group norms
Time Needed	20–30 minutes
Room Arrangement	Small groups
Difficulty Level	Higher risk, easy to do
Brain Bits	Emotional impact and social support, development of cognitive learning in terms of developing common vocabulary, clarifying, and sharing
Brain's Natural Learning Systems	Physical, cognitive, reflective, social
Adult Learning Principle	Experiential: connects to what we know and do well Life application: determines real-life use and process of transfer to participants' unique circumstances
Materials	Chart paper and markers

Process Directions

1. In each group, a recorder is identified.
2. Each person in the groups thinks about and jots down one or two things that are important to him or her when working in a group, such as "Everyone is on time," "While we're together, we listen to the speaker."
3. In turn, going around the table, each person states his or her expectation.
4. The recorder jots expectations down on the chart paper as stated.
5. When all ideas are recorded, there is time for questions and checking for clarification about each item.

6. Some items may be reworded or coupled or condensed with others.

7. After the clarification phase is finished, each member of the group gets to rank the norms using colored self-sticking dots, which are given a ranking score number or a rank order such as 5 for the highest priority ranking to 1 for the least important.

8. The dots or numbers are totaled, and those norms with the highest priority become the norms for the group (generally four to seven are used).

9. Participants agree to these and feel a commitment to them as they have created them personally.

10. It is each group member's job to enforce them on behalf of the group.

When

- Participants need some active involvement related to their own well-being.
- People need clarity about how they will work together.
- Dialogue and creating consensus are necessary.
- There is a need for team building and perspective taking.

Examples and Uses

1. This may be used to establish group norms.

2. It is also a process to prioritize goals.

3. It may be used to rank and come to consensus about any number of issues including student behavior.

Selected References

Daniels (1986), Johnson and Johnson (1991), Johnson and Johnson (1994), Kagan (1992), Kassouf (1970), Van de Ven and Delbecq (1974).

Norms for our group:

1. We start and end on time.
2. We listen with respect.
3. We share the leadership and facilitation of the group.
4. We criticize ideas, not people.
5. We're open to new ideas.

STRATEGY 12

Personal, Interpersonal, Task Model (P.I.T.)

Purpose: Creating a Growth-Oriented Climate

People often rush into meetings coming from very hectic situations. Participants need time to decompress before the work begins. P.I.T. is a strategy to help in that decompression process and to re-energize people to focus and take on new ideas and challenges. It also values individuals and their personal issues and shows empathy as a collective group.

Basics

Number of Participants	May be done in small table groups or partners
Time Needed	5–6 minutes
Room Arrangement	Table groups
Difficulty Level	Low risk, easy
Brain Bits	Emotional impact and social support, development of cognitive learning in terms of developing common vocabulary, clarifying, and sharing
Brain's Natural Learning Systems	Emotional, reflective, social
Adult Learning Principle	Experiential: connects to what we know and do well Life application: determines real-life use and process of transfer to participants' unique circumstances
Materials	None P. I. T. on poster or PowerPoint slide

Process Directions

1. **Personal:** Participants take a minute to think about how they are feeling and what has been successful or challenging that day, or about something that is going in their lives that they would be willing to share.

2. **Interpersonal:** Everyone shares their thoughts with the others or a partner. Colleagues acknowledge and show appreciation and empathy as appropriate.

3. **Task:** The task for the session is identified or the agenda is built, and the team begins the work.

When

- Participants need to feel that their own well-being is important.
- The group needs active involvement of personal ideas and feelings.
- Dialogue and creating connections are necessary for team development.
- There is a need for team building.

Examples and Uses

1. It could be that P.I.T. becomes routine at the beginning of each meeting.

2. It would be especially important during stressful times when people need encouragement or support.

Selected References

Costa and Garmston (2002), Daniels (1986), Gibbs (2001), Hargreaves and Dawe (1989), Johnson and Johnson (1991, 1994), Kagan (1992), Robertson and Kagan (1992).

Personal

Interpersonal

Task

Tests

Scoring tools

After considering strategies others used, what can I add to my repertoire to inform me about how my students are learning?

STRATEGY 13

Processing Pause

Purpose: Creating a Growth-Oriented Climate

This strategy is used to get participants' voices in the room even with larger groups or to note learning from start of session to the end of session. This is great for creating a simple processing break.

Basics

Number of Participants	May be done in small table groups or as individuals and then share
Time Needed	10–15 minutes
Room Arrangement	Table groups
Difficulty Level	Low risk, easy
Brain Bits	Emotional impact and social support, development of cognitive learning in terms of developing common vocabulary, clarifying, and sharing Activates long-term memory potential with visual representation, discussion, and determination of transfer of new information
Adult Learning Principle	Experiential: connects to what we know and do well Life application: determines real-life use and process of transfer to participants' unique circumstances
Materials	Template

Process Directions

1. Have participants fill out the template after hearing a portion of a presentation or after the team has discussed a topic for a period of time.
2. Share one or more parts with your table group or partner.
3. Share multiple items with whole group.
4. With points of confusion, ask for clarification from the facilitator or answer at each table group.
5. "Park" key ideas by telling the small group how you will use the information you found most important and when you will use it.

When

- Participants need to make meaning from new learning.
- Participants need a break from a discussion to personalize what the implications are for them.

- The group needs some clarifying of solutions and problem solving to note the best ideas for the individual or team.

Examples and Uses

1. Use at the start of the second half of a workshop to help participants make meaning of or prioritize learning for better transfer.

2. Use as a processing pause at the end of learning or a team session.

3. Use as a processing tool after a protocol such as "the Interview."

4. Use to document the work of a team for that session or series of sessions. This is an alternative to logging or journaling progress.

5. Use to help participants when the learning is dense, is complex, or requires personalization for better transfer.

Selected References

Hartzler and Henry (1994); Hoffman and Olson-Ness (1996); Marzano, Norford, Paynter, Gaddy, and Pickering (2004).

Processing Pause

Information or Ideas Worth Noting	Graphic Representation
Questions or Points of Confusion	
Summary of Key Ideas From Discussion	

STRATEGY 14

Random Partners

Purpose: Creating a Growth-Oriented Climate

In professional learning communities, it is important to connect everyone with everyone else. Learners of all ages need dialogue to explore and clarify information so that it can become knowledge.

Basics

Number of Participants	Any number will work. You may have to do a little juggling to make sure everyone has a partner for each appointment time
Time Needed	10–15 minutes
Room Arrangement	Sufficient floor to walk about and meet up with your partner
Difficulty Level	Low risk, easy
Brain Bits	Emotional impact and social support, development of cognitive learning in terms of developing common vocabulary, movement suits our need for physical interaction
Brain's Natural Learning Systems	Social, emotional, physical, cognitive, reflective
Adult Learning Principle	Experiential: connects to what we know and do well Life application: determines real-life use and process of transfer to participants' unique circumstances
Materials	Appointment cards

Process Directions

1. Prepare appointment cards, such as small 4" × 4" cards with a symbol for each season such as a snowman, beach scene, blossoms, and autumn leaves.

2. People will put their name on their appointment card.

3. Then everyone will walk around and make appointments for each of the seasons.

4. As a person meets another person, he or she will write the partner's name on the appointment card at the season when they plan to meet.

5. Each will thank the partner and move on to make another appointment with someone else at a different season time.

6. When the participants have four appointments (winter, spring, summer, and fall), they will go back to their table.

7. The facilitator can then use the appointment cards to get people together for a discussion or a task at any time during the day, meeting, or workshop.

When

- Use after lunch, at the end of the morning, or at the end of the day.
- Use any time people need a change of state and another colleague to discuss an idea.
- The group needs to energize through movement and discussion.
- People need to move or get up.
- The facilitator needs to lower the risk for participation.
- Multiple viewpoints would help problem solve or plan.
- One conversation at a time makes it safer than whole-group processing.

Examples and Uses

1. After a video clip ask the following prompt using this group format: "How might you use the strategy exhibited in the video with your students or in your content area?"

2. Meet with your spring partner and chat about how you will . . . ?

3. What suggestions do you have to remove roadblocks to . . . ?

4. Use partners to read an article and discuss the key points.

5. You may be creative and use appointment cards with special significance to the group, such as seasonal symbols for Halloween, sports events, holidays, and so forth.

6. Clock partners are great and give 12 appointments, but you may want to have people line up in two lines facing each other, and then first the person across will be the one o'clock partner. One line moves to the right with the end person coming to the other end of the line. The new person across in the other line will be the two o'clock partner. The line continues to move until all 12 appointments are made.

Selected References

Daniels (1986), Hargreaves and Dawe (1989), Johnson and Johnson (1991, 1994), Kagan (1992), Robertson and Kagan (1992), Sousa (2004), Wellman and Lipton (2003).

Find a partner

Spring _____

Winter _____

Summer _____

Fall _____

_____

Clock Partners

1:00 _____

2:00 _____

3:00 _____

4:00 _____

5:00 _____

6:00 _____

7:00 _____

8:00 _____

9:00 _____

10:00 _____

11:00 _____

12:00 _____

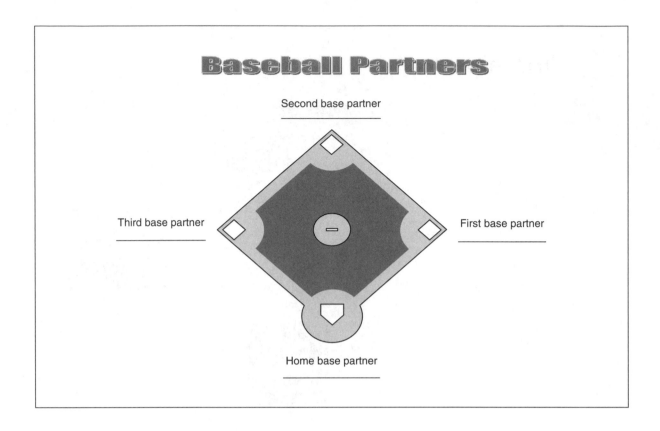

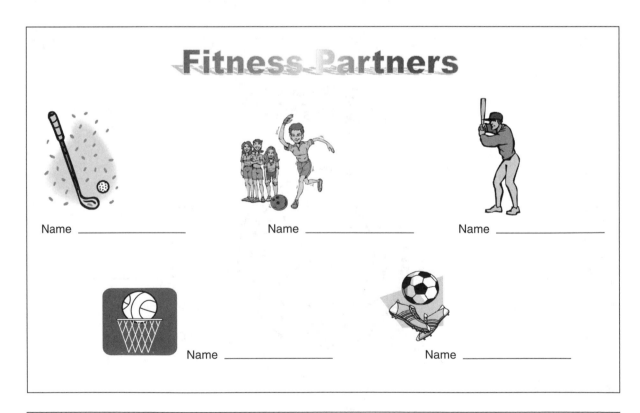

STRATEGY 15

Synectics

Purpose: Creating a Growth-Oriented Climate

William Gordon created the notion of Synectics as a process for creative thinking. It helps people understand a more abstract concept by linking it to something they already know. It taps into both hemispheres of the brain and stretches their thinking.

Basics

Number of Participants	May be done individually, in small table groups, or as a large group
Time Needed	10–15 minutes
Room Arrangement	Table groups
Difficulty Level	Low risk, easy
Brain Bits	Emotional impact and social support, development of cognitive learning in terms of developing common vocabulary, clarifying, and sharing Creative thinking and novelty helpful in learning
Brain's Natural Learning Systems	Social, emotional, cognitive, physical, reflective
Adult Learning Principle	Experiential: connects to what we know and do well Life application: determines real-life use and process of transfer to participants' unique circumstances
Materials	Chart paper or newsprint and colored markers

Process Directions

1. Create a clear understanding of a concept such as differentiation, authentic assessment, quality teaching, or teamwork.

2. The person or group chooses something they know very well to which they can relate the more abstract or new concept, such as a roller coaster, box of chocolates, or journey.

3. In the spirit of cooperative learning, assign group members a role to play:
   a. Writer
   b. Clarifier
   c. Encourager
   d. Materials manager

4. The writer will write: "Differentiation is like…" at the top of the chart. Team members will brainstorm all the reasons or connections that the two items have in common.

5. All the group members contribute ideas that connect the more abstract concept to the more familiar one, such as by creating a symbol on the page to represent the analogy.

When

- Participants need some active involvement related to concept clarification.
- People need a change of state and another colleague to discuss an idea.
- The facilitator needs to lower the risk for participation.
- Dialogue and creating consensus are necessary.
- There is a need for team building.

Examples and Uses

1. Participants need to understand a complex concept by putting it in their own words and relating it to something they already know about.

2. The strategy can be used to deepen thinking around a controversial topic such as implementing problem-based math.

3. Participants may be able to infer relationships that help them transfer newly learned concepts or skills to the classroom.

4. This strategy can add humor to a complex topic.

Selected References

Gordon (1961), Marzano et al. (2004), Roukes (1988).

Examples

A well-functioning team is like *sailing a ship* **because:**

Each member has a job to do.

The destination is clear to all members.

Each person brings different talents to the process.

Sometimes it's smooth sailing; sometimes it's rough waters.

Sometimes it is full sail; sometimes we run out of wind.

Storms erupt; seas calm again.

We can get off course.

DIFFERENTIATION IS LIKE . . .

USING DATA IS LIKE . . .

TEACHING IS LIKE . . .

STRATEGY 16

T Chart and Y Chart

Purpose: Creating a Growth-Oriented Climate

When establishing working norms for team success, people often need to clarify what is important to them and clarify behaviors. These charts are also a tool for organizing information and facilitating dialogue.

Basics

Number of Participants	May be done in small table groups or as a large group
Time Needed	10–15 minutes
Room Arrangement	Table groups
Difficulty Level	Low risk, easy
Brain Bits	Emotional impact and social support, development of cognitive learning in terms of developing common vocabulary, clarifying, and sharing
Brain's Natural Learning Systems	Emotional, social, physical, cognitive, reflective
Adult Learning Principle	Experiential: connects to what we know and do well

Life application: determines real-life use and process of transfer to participants' unique circumstances |
| Materials | Chart paper and markers |

Process Directions

1. Create a T on a sheet of chart paper at each table.

2. Put a title on the page to focus the thinking. One might be "Well-Functioning Teams."

3. Label the left side "Looks Like." Label the right side "Sounds Like."

4. Ask participants to consider what a well-functioning team would look like as it worked well and what it would sound like when it worked well.

5. After some thinking and discussion time, ask participants to contribute ideas that can be written on the common chart.

6. Doing this at each table would give people more "air time" and input.

7. Charts can then be posted and perused by participants to look for commonalities.

8. Another large group chart can be created by the whole group after the initial charts are completed and posted.

9. This could become the shared vision of a well-functioning team.

When

- Participants need some active involvement related to their own well-being.
- People need a change of state and another colleague to discuss an idea.
- People need to move or get up.
- The facilitator needs to lower the risk for participation.
- Dialogue and creating consensus are necessary.
- There is a need for team building.

Examples and Uses

1. Using "Looks like . . . sounds like" can create a clear understanding of a concept.

2. This helps clarify what a concept is or is not.

3. It helps to compare and contrast two concepts, such as a differentiated classroom versus a traditional classroom.

4. May be used with headings such as cause and effect related to a topic.

Selected References

Enchanted Learning (2006a, 2006b); English and Dean (2004); Hill and Hancock (1993); Johnson and Johnson (1991); Johnson, Johnson, and Johnson-Holubec (1993); Gregory (2000).

Examples of T Charts

A Well-Functioning Team

Looks Like	Sounds Like

Compare and Contrast

Differentiated Classroom	Traditional Classroom

Differentiating Instruction . . .

Is	Is Not

School Behavior

Cause	Effect

Y-Chart Examples

A Y chart is a variation of the T chart. It adds the dimension of emotions to the mix. It would push people to think about feelings associated with the concept. What would it look like, sound like, and feel like? Tapping into human emotions helps people internalize information and develop empathy for others, which will create a safe and growth-oriented climate. A Y chart can also be used to organize information for any idea or concept that has three parts. It would work with the jigsaw technique. Each person reads and summarizes part of an article. You could give participants roles so that they rotate roles as they explain and record their parts. The roles that might be used could be Reporter, Recorder, and Clarifier. That way everyone is engaged at each step.

A Well-Functioning Team

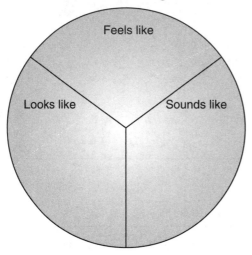

How do we serve diverse learners?

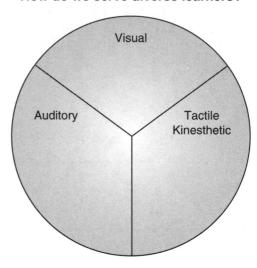

Whose responsibility is it?

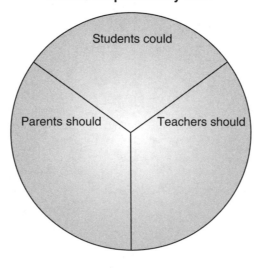

Sharing Knowledge and Skills

If schools want to enhance their organizational capacity to boost student learning, they should work on building professional community that is characterized by shared purpose, collaborative activity, and collective responsibility among school staff.

—Newmann and Wehlage (1995)

THE AGE OF ACCOUNTABILITY

In this age of high accountability, it is essential that we ban together to better plan for success for all. Digging deeper into data can be a great place to start for collaborative teams. A shared purpose of helping every learner succeed is a vision that enables professional learning communities to stay the course and open up their classrooms, practice, and expertise to others. It is essential that the teachers' knowledge of curriculum and instruction is up to date and carefully aligned. Just as important is the increased toolkit teachers need to meet the diverse needs of students. Just getting results on high-stakes assessments is not enough; we also need to prepare students for an unknown future in the twenty-first century. We are accountable for increasing our knowledge and skills to accomplish these tasks. There is so much to learn that we need to prioritize what we take on, and we need to do this together. Together we can accomplish more on behalf of our students and take a huge weight off teachers. Working as a team, the work is achievable. Working as individuals, the new accountability can be overwhelming.

HABITUATING WHAT WE LEARN

We have long known that change takes time, patience, and perseverance. Habitual practice hard-wires procedures in the cerebellum, and behaviors and skills become unconscious as we execute them. If we want to change those behaviors, we must undo that wiring or circuitry and rewire in a new way so the new behavior becomes the modus operandi. The research at McRel tells us that it takes 24 perfect practice trials to reach 80% mastery. This is why change often fails. The repetitions are too tedious, are too awkward, and create feelings of inadequacy. When the going gets tough, more often than not, we quit, as it just requires too much effort to carry on. With supportive colleagues, we are more likely to "keep on keepin' on." Professional learning communities offer the support, sharing, and problem solving necessary to sustain the initiative and accomplish the changes necessary.

COMMUNITIES OF LEARNERS

Roland Barth suggests profound learning in true communities of learners is fostered by the following:

- Acknowledging one's inadequacies
- Posing one's own problems
- Risk taking
- Humor
- Collaboration with other learners
- Compassion
- Modeling
- The presence of a moral purpose

Michael Fullan (2002) says that we turn information and skills into knowledge through dialogue, discussion, and self-reflection. He also suggests that in schools, we need to focus on change, collaboration, and celebration.

Bennett, Joyce, and Showers (2002) gave us real insight into what makes a difference in adult learning through quality and varied staff development practices that increase student achievement. They examined the levels of impact of staff development, including the following:

- Awareness, skill development and application, and problem solving related to the components of training;
- Presentation of theory;
- Modeling;
- Practice and low-risk feedback; and
- Collaborative coaching, study teams, and peer visits.

Without the sharing, support, and problem solving teams offer, implementation is not really achieved and long-term change accomplished.

Relationship Between Levels of Impact and Components of Training

Level of Impact/ Components of Training	Awareness Plus Concept Understanding	Skill Attainment	Application and Problem Solving
Presentation of Theory	85%	18%	5% to 10%
Modeling	85%	18%	5% to 10%
Practice and Low-Risk Feedback	85%	80%	10% to 15%
Coaching, Student Teams, and Peer Visits	90%	90%	80% to 90%

From Bennett, Joyce, and Showers (2002).

PRIMARY PURPOSE FOR THE STRATEGIES IN THIS SECTION

In this chapter, we offer you strategies to expand the knowledge and skills conducive to growth that support

- Expanding the toolkit
- Developing strategies
- Transferring
- Expanding options
- Impacting results

STRATEGY 17

Four-Corner Cards

Purpose: Sharing Knowledge and Skills

This strategy could be used as a conversation starter or preassessment. It allows people to begin with their knowledge and questions and allows them to share these in a semiprivate environment one on one.

Basics

Number of Participants	Any number
Time Needed	10–15 minutes
Room Arrangement	Space to move around
Difficulty Level	Low risk, easy
Brain Bits	Emotional impact and social support, development of cognitive learning in terms of developing common vocabulary, clarifying, and sharing
Brain's Natural Learning Systems	Emotional, reflective, social
Adult Learning Principle	Experiential: connects to what we know and do well Life application: determines real-life use and process of transfer to participants' unique circumstances
Materials	Advanced organizer, pen

Process Directions

1. Give participants a card with four sections and four prompts.

2. Each person responds to the prompts in each corner of the card.

3. When all are finished, they can walk about and share their four corners with four other participants.

4. This also sets the stage for professional development responding to the needs of staff.

5. It can also be used for brainstorming purposes as with the life preservers shown.

6. The life preserver can be drawn on a large piece of newsprint, and four participants can use colored markers to brainstorm in their own section.

When

- Participants need some active involvement related to their own well-being.
- People need a change of state and another colleague to discuss an idea.
- People need to move or get up.
- The facilitator needs to lower the risk for participation.
- Dialogue and creating consensus are necessary.
- There is a need for team building.

Selected Reference

Gibbs (2001), Hill and Hill (1990), Hoffman and Olson-Ness (1996), Reid (2002).

EXAMPLES AND USES

Related to assessment practices, the card may look like this:

What assessment tools have you used this week?	Why are assessments important to you for planning?
How would you explain authentic assessment?	What would you like to know more about related to assessment?

Facilitating a conversation about English-Language Learner students:

How do you accommodate English-Language Learner (ELL) students?	What would you like to know about ELL?
What aspects might especially difficult in your subject area?	Do you have any resources that help you with ELL students?

A life preserver is another form of Four-Corner Cards. It may be used for brainstorming or preassessment.

The life preserver can be divided into as many sections as there are people in the group.

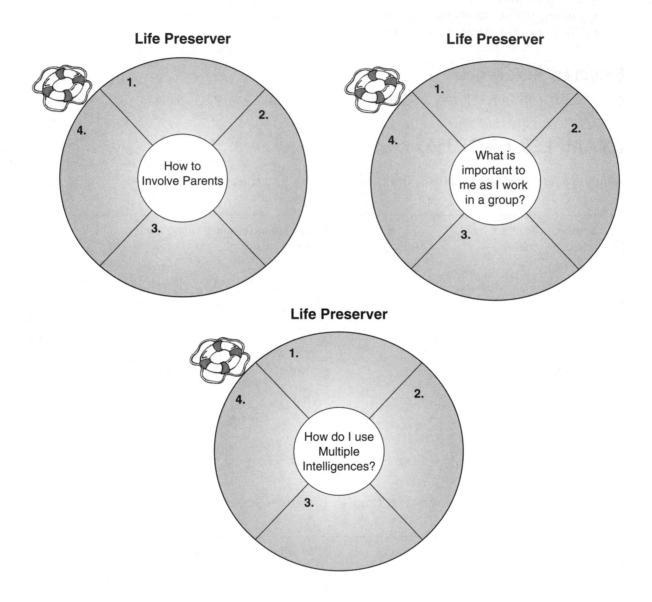

STRATEGY 18

Inside-Outside Circles

Purpose: Sharing Knowledge and Skills

"Inside-outside circles" is a process that helps teams process and reflect on new ideas, while checking out various points of view in a safe conversation setting. It is inclusive of all participants and decreases resistance to problem solving and increases openness to the ideas of others.

Basics

Number of Participants	At least three in each circle
Time Needed	10–15 minutes (variables include number of moves and depth of prompts)
Room Arrangement	Sufficient floor space to stand in circles
Difficulty Level	Low risk, easy
Brain Bits	Emotional impact and social support, development of cognitive learning in terms of developing common vocabulary, movement suits our need for physical interaction
Brain's Natural Learning Systems	Social, emotional, cognitive, reflective, physical
Adult Learning Principle	Experiential: connects to what we know and do well Life application: determines real-life use and process of transfer to participants' unique circumstances
Materials	None, except personal notes or advanced organizers
Other	Facilitator walking around to monitor time between rotations and to avoid participants getting bored or off-task conversation

Process Directions

1. Put several people in a circle facing outward—more than three.
2. Put an equal number of people in an outer circle, each one facing one person in the inner circle.
3. Give participants a prompt that encourages reflection or application of thinking.
4. The inside person speaks first.
5. The outside person responds.
6. Each outside circle person moves two places (people) clockwise.

7. Repeat Steps 4, 5, and 6 one or two more times depending on the size of circles.

8. You can also change the order of who talks or responds first.

When

- This is good after lunch, at the end of the morning, or at the end of the day.
- People need a change of state and another colleague to discuss an idea.
- People need to move or get up.
- The facilitator needs to lower the risk for participation.
- Multiple viewpoints would help problem solve or plan.
- There is a need for team building.
- One conversation at a time makes it safer than whole-group processing.

Examples and Uses

After a video clip, ask one of the following prompts using the group format:

1. "How might you use the strategy exhibited in the video with your students or in your content area?"

2. What are some strategies you use to motivate reluctant learners?

3. What suggestions do you have to remove roadblocks to . . . ?

4. What do you do with your English-Language Learners to assist with vocabulary acquisition?

5. What is a creative note-taking strategy that you use with your students?

Selected References

Annenberg Institute for School Reform (1998); Australian Government Department of Education (2006); Chadwick (2006); Gibbs (2001); Johnson, Johnson, and Johnson-Holubec (1993); Kagan (1992).

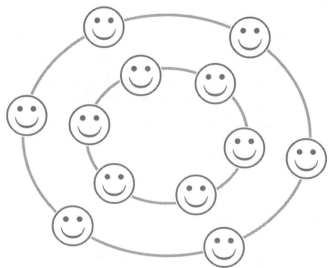

STRATEGY 19

Jigsaw

Purpose: Sharing Knowledge and Skills

There are three types of jigsaw that can be used to process information and facilitate dialogue.

Simple Jigsaw Square: You may use a simple jigsaw square of three, four, or five people. Each person must become knowledgeable about one piece of information in a table group and then teach the new information to the rest of the group.

Expert Jigsaw: This is similar to the simple jigsaw, except each expert from all the groups will join together with the other experts to discuss the material before teaching it back to the original group.

Table Jigsaw: Each table is responsible for a different piece of content. Each table studies the material and decides how to teach it to the large group.

Basics

Number of Participants	May be done in small table groups of three, four, or five
Time Needed	20–30 minutes
Room Arrangement	Table groups
Difficulty Level	Low risk, moderately difficult
Brain Bits	Emotional impact and social support, development of cognitive learning in terms of developing common vocabulary, clarifying, and sharing
Brain's Natural Learning Systems	Social, emotional, cognitive, physical, reflective
Adult Learning Principle	Experiential: connects to what we know and do well Life application: determines real-life use and process of transfer to participants' unique circumstances
Materials	Advanced organizer

Process Directions
Simple Jigsaw Square

1. Each group is formed with several members. Each person letters off: A, B, C, or D. Each person in the group has a particular part to become expert with and to share with the group of four.

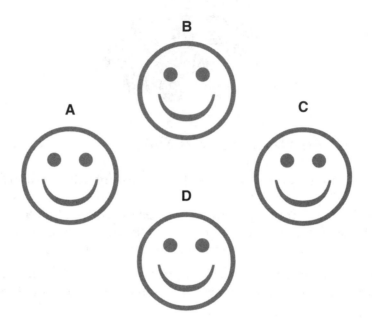

Process Directions
Expert Jigsaw

1. Each group is formed with several members. Each person letters off: A, B, C, or D. This is the base group.

2. After each person has a letter, a part of the reading, article, chapter, or overall task is assigned to each person.

3. Then all the A's, B's, C's, and D's meet as four new groups to read, discuss, or complete their part of the task. Direct people to four corners of the room (A, B, C, D) to do their expert task.

4. When the task is complete or material is learned, the experts return to their base group to share their part of the jigsaw.

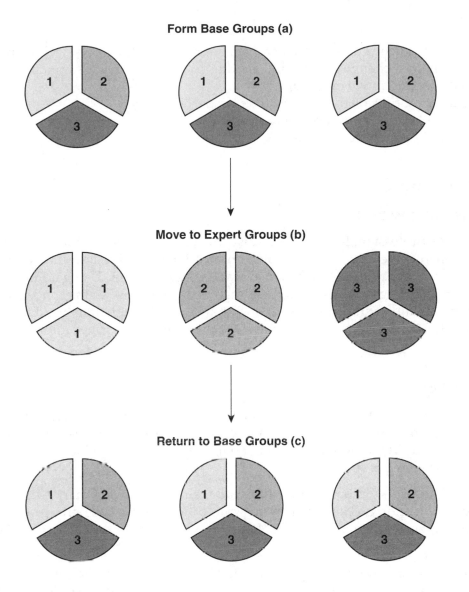

Process Directions

Table Jigsaw

1. Instead of each person in the group lettering off and going off to an expert group, the entire group becomes an expert and presents their part to the other groups.

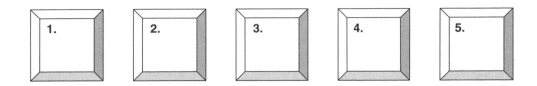

When

- Participants need some active involvement related to their own well-being.
- People need a change of state and another colleague to discuss an idea.
- People need to move or get up.
- The facilitator needs to lower the risk for participation.
- Dialogue and creating consensus are necessary.
- There is a need for team building.

Examples and Uses

1. Simple Jigsaw Square

Sometimes professional reading can be difficult in the rush of the day for educators. Using a jigsaw can be a way of facilitating professional reading and initiating a dialogue about important aspects of research and educational innovations. Using a simple square can be a way of initiating that discussion through acquiring, discussing, and contemplating ideas and information and turning them into knowledge through dialogue. Each person will read or watch a part of the article or video and then share his or her information with the table group.

2. Expert Jigsaw

Step 1. When teachers are reading a book for a book study, you may have four or five people in each group. They would letter off: A, B, C, D, E. This is the base or home group. People would divide up a chapter in equal or appropriate sections for the four or five people in the group.

Step 2. All the A's would meet together, read their part, and summarize key points. Then they would decide on the best way to share or teach their base group what they have become expert in. Similarly, B's, C's, D's, and E's would do the same with their content or section.

Step 3. The base or home group would reconvene, and each person in turn would share his or her part with the other members. An advance organizer could be used so each person can capture the key points of each section.

3. Table Jigsaw

This strategy can also be used to view a video with each table group looking for specific information as to one aspect of the concept being explored. For example, while watching a video about using data for instructional decisions, each table group using an advanced organizer can collect information about

Why?   What?   How?   When?

Why?	What?
How?	**When?**

Selected References

Aronson, Blaney, Stephin, Sikes, and Snapp (1978); Bennett, Rolheiser, and Stevahn (1991); Hertz-Lazarowitz, Kagan, Sharan, Slavin, and Webb (1985); Hill and Hill (1990), Johnson et al. (1993); Slavin (1994).

STRATEGY 20

Know, Want to Know, Learned (KWL)

Purpose: Sharing Knowledge and Skills

"KWL" helps staff focus on the desired result. It helps clarify what has been learned and what needs to be learned. It also helps prioritize the work to get to that result. In addition, teams can use this for early sharing of knowledge and skills.

Basics

Number of Participants	Three to 8 in small groups or a larger group of 30 to 40
Time Needed	20 minutes
Room Arrangement	Tables and chairs for small groups
Difficulty Level	Low risk, easy
Brain Bits	Emotional impact and social support, development of cognitive learning in terms of developing common vocabulary, helps with prioritization
Adult Learning Principle	Experiential: connects to what we know and do well and to what we want to accomplish Life application: determines real-life use and process of transfer to participants' unique circumstances Self-directed: opportunities to prioritize are essential
Materials	Three pieces of chart paper for Know, Want to Know, Learned or template letter–size paper for each table group
Other	A two-part process, a great opening and closing to learning either in a single meeting or over the course of several meetings

Process Directions

1. For one large group, hang up three pieces of chart paper labeled "Know," "Want to Know," and "Learned."

2. The facilitator asks the group what they already know about a topic or issue and records their brainstormed ideas.

3. Then the facilitator asks what the group wants to learn and records their answer.

4. At the conclusion of the learning, brainstorm again and ask what participants learned.

When

- Use at the start of new learning or a new project and to reflect on that learning and the results afterward.
- Use when working on a single task or specific step in a longer process.
- Use when contemplating how to use new learning in your classroom or work setting.
- There are many ideas for "Want to Know" and this may help your prioritize.
- Use if trying to get a team to focus on desired results of learning.

Examples and Uses

1. We are going to read a book about the strategies needed to improve student achievement. What do we already know? What do we want to know? Then we will record what we learned that was especially promising given our situation.

2. Before we view this video, we will fill in the first two columns. After the film, we will capture the learning we want to remember.

3. What do we know about effective lessons? What do we want to learn from each other? Then in a couple of months, we will describe what we learned and want to incorporate into future planning.

Selected References

Graphic Organizer (2006), North Central Regional Educational Laboratory (NCREL, 2006), Ogle (1986).

KWL

Topic:

K	W	L
What Do We Know?	**What Do We Want to Know?**	**What Did We Learn?**

VARIATIONS ON KWL

K What Do We Know?	W Why Do We Want to Know This?	L How Will We Use What We Have Learned?

K What Strategies Do We Know Work for Our Students Now?	W What Strategies Do We Want to Learn About?	L Under What Circumstances Would We Use These Newly Learned Strategies?

STRATEGY 21

Perspective Lens

Purpose: Sharing Knowledge and Skills

Using a perspective lens is a critical thinking strategy that can be used to more deeply analyze a situation or critique ideas or strategies that may be implemented.

Basics

Number of Participants	May be done in small table groups of six where each participant has a lens or as a large group where each table views the situation with a different lens
Time Needed	10–15 minutes
Room Arrangement	Table groups
Difficulty Level	Low risk, easy
Brain Bits	Emotional impact and social support, development of cognitive learning in terms of developing common vocabulary, clarifying, and sharing
Brain's Natural Learning Systems	Emotional, reflective, social
Adult Learning Principle	Experiential: connects to what we know and do well Life application: determines real-life use and process of transfer to participants' unique circumstances
Materials	Chart paper and markers

Process Directions

1. Each person in a six-person group is assigned to a particular lens, or each table is assigned to one of the lenses. If there are more than six tables, just continue to assign lenses until each table has one. It doesn't matter if there are multiples as long as each lens is assigned.

2. View a video of a classroom strategy or read an article and jot down ideas from their lens's perspective.

3. Each person will share in turn.

4. Follow up with a general discussion related to the topic or strategy using the perspectives as a way to get a well-rounded understanding of the issue.

When

- Participants need some active involvement related to their own well-being.
- People need a change of state and another colleague to discuss an idea.
- People need to move or get up.
- The facilitator needs to lower the risk for participation.
- Dialogue and creating consensus are necessary.
- There is a need for team building.

Examples and Uses

1. Using the following chart, participants can look at a topic that is new to the group and is up for consideration in implementation by the team.

2. Each lens is assigned either individually in a six-person group or by table.

3. Teachers read an article or watch a video showing the differentiated classroom.

4. After the activity, the chart can be filled in.

5. If done as a small group, each person can share his or her perspective with the other members of the group.

6. If done as a large room, each table can report on their perspective.

7. Then a large group discussion will follow.

Selected References

Beaudoin and Taylor (2004), De Bono (1987), Gregory (2006), Hill and Hill (1990), Hoffman and Olson-Ness (1996).

Thinking Lenses

White Lens Pure white facts	Just the facts! Information Details Truths Computer-like	
Purple Lens Judgment	The down side! What's wrong? Why it won't work Errors or mistakes	
Red Lens Just feel it	How do you feel? Emotions Get it out there Hunches Opinion	
Green Lens Green and growing	Where can this go? Growth Creative New "seeds"	
Yellow Lens Sunshine, brightness	Look on the bright side! Positive Up side Constructive Possibilities	
Blue Lens Cool and control	Pulling things together? Thinking about thinking Director of thinking Summaries	

STRATEGY 22

Pluses and Wishes

Purpose: Sharing Knowledge and Skills

When desiring feedback at the end of working session, this is useful in getting people to be positive and constructive about the process as they work together.

Basics

Number of Participants	May be done individually (as a ticket out), in small table groups, or as a large group
Time Needed	5–10 minutes
Room Arrangement	Any
Difficulty Level	Low risk, easy
Brain Bits	Emotional impact and social support, development of cognitive learning in terms of developing common vocabulary, clarifying, and sharing
Adult Learning Principle	Experiential: connects to what we know and do well Life application: determines real-life use and process of transfer to participants' unique circumstances
Materials	Chart paper and markers, index cards, self-sticking notes, or printed cards as figure

Process Directions

1. Give each participant a form or sticky note to use.

2. On the left side, ask each to list all the positives or "pluses" about the meeting or workshop.

3. On the right side, ask each to make helpful suggestions for the next day or meeting or time they will work together.

4. Collect these and share them as data the next time the group meets.

5. Try to incorporate some of the helpful suggestions to improve the quality of the next experience based on the feedback and requests of the participants.

6. Having people use individual positives is a safe way for people to be open and honest in their reflections.

7. As the group becomes more trusting, this could be done as a large group, sharing successes and suggesting helpful considerations for the next encounter.

When

- Participants need some active involvement related to their own well-being.
- It is important to the group to celebrate successes and collectively consider needs for the next session.

Examples and Uses

1. This strategy is a way of considering accomplishments and goals. It facilitates reflection on process and progress.

2. At the end of a meeting, participants brainstorm pluses that have occurred during the session and wishes or requests for the next time the team meets.

Selected References

Colan (2003), Costa and Garmston (2002), Garmston and Wellman (1999), Robbins (1991), Mind Tools (2006a, 2006b, 2006c).

Pluses	Wishes
We were very productive today.	We need to meet more often to work on assessments.
Everyone was on time.	
We were focused and concentrated on the task to be done.	We should collect examples of student work to further assess their needs collectively.
It was refreshing to work together to accomplish our goal.	We need to work together to create more authentic assessments for students.
I feel we are better prepared to plan with the data we examined.	

PLUS, MINUS, DELTA

Plus, Minus, Delta is a process that can be used similarly to Pluses and Wishes but includes three steps: Pluses, Minuses, and Changes Needed.

Use this simple organizer as a reflection at the end of the session that might be used as a ticket out.

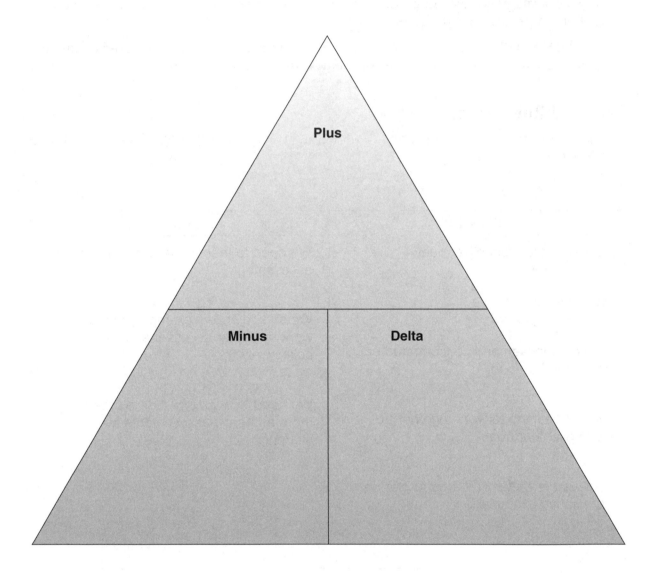

A Plus for Today

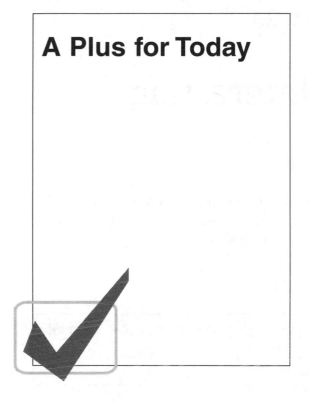

A Wish for Tomorrow

A Plus for Today's Meeting

A Wish for the Next Meeting

Plus, Minus, Interesting

Purpose: Sharing Knowledge and Skills

This strategy is extremely useful for group discussion that looks at an issue from several perspectives of what might be Plus or Positive about the issue, what might be Minus or Negative about the issue, and what might be Interesting about the idea.

Basics

Number of Participants	May be done as individuals, in small table, groups or as a large group
Time Needed	10–15 minutes
Room Arrangement	Table groups
Difficulty Level	Low risk, easy
Brain Bits	Emotional impact and social support, development of cognitive learning in terms of developing common vocabulary, clarifying, and sharing
Brain's Natural Learning Systems	Cognitive, reflective
Adult Learning Principle	Experiential: connects to what we know and do well
	Life application: determines real-life use and process of transfer to participants' unique circumstances
Materials	Chart paper and markers or advance organizer as the following chart

Process Directions

1. Present an issue for scrutiny or watch a video.

2. Work alone, with a partner, or in a small group.

3. Use the chart or chart paper and fill in what is a Plus, a Minus, or Interesting.

When

- Use as decisions need to be made about an issue.
- We need to scrutinize an idea from multiple perspectives.
- Critical thinking is needed.

Selected References

De Bono (1987), Mind Tools (2006a, 2006b, 2006c), Texas Department of Education (2006).

Examples and Uses

1. Staff or a team are debating an issue to make a decision. To fully look at all angles and points of view, Plus, Minus, or Interesting can be applied: "Let's look at implementing a block schedule in our school."

Plus	Minus	Interesting

2. The team has just watched a video of a new instructional strategy such as cubing. They meet with a partner and use the chart to fill in what is a Plus, a Minus, and Interesting.

3. Sometimes you may want to use prompts to help with the processing. The following prompts might prove useful.

Plus

I like this idea for the following reasons . . .

This seems to agree with what I already know or do . . .

This helps me see or understand . . .

Minus

I don't agree with this because . . .

This just doesn't fit well with what I know about . . .

I have some concerns about . . .

Interesting

I had never thought about that before but . . .

I see where I could adapt . . .

This gives me a new slant on the topic . . .

Upside, On Side, Downside: This is a variation of Plus, Minus, Interesting looking at the upside of the idea, how you are already on side with the concept, and what might be the downside or aspects you need to pay attention to in implementation.

UPSIDE, ON SIDE, DOWNSIDE

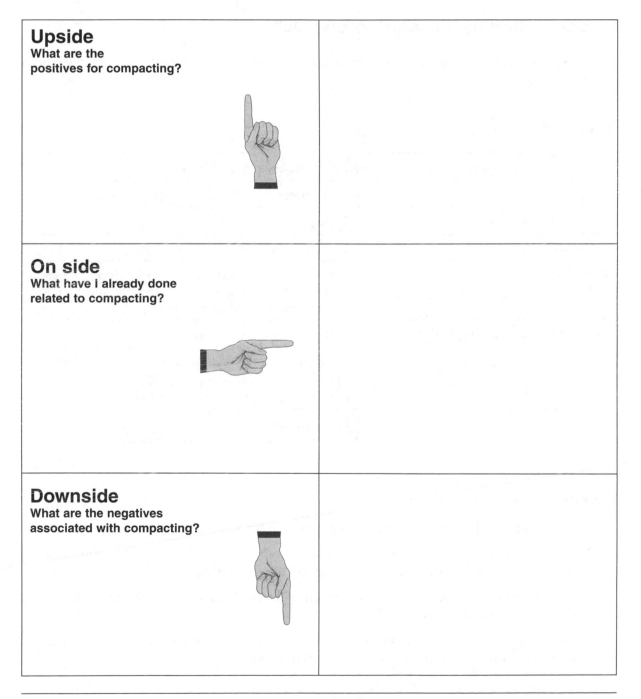

Upside
What are the
positives for compacting?

On side
What have I already done
related to compacting?

Downside
What are the negatives
associated with compacting?

STRATEGY 24

Promissory Note

Purpose: Sharing Knowledge and Skills

A promissory note can be used to help facilitate transfer of ideas or skills into the classroom or schoolhouse.

Basics

Number of Participants	Any number, activity done individually
Time Needed	5–7 minutes
Room Arrangement	Table groups
Difficulty Level	Low risk, easy
Brain Bits	Emotional impact and social support, development of cognitive learning in terms of developing common vocabulary, clarifying, and sharing
Brain's Natural Learning Systems	Reflective, emotional, cognitive
Adult Learning Principle	Experiential: connects to what we know and do well Life application: determines real-life use and process of transfer to participants' unique circumstances
Materials	Paper and envelopes

Process Directions

1. Give each participant a sheet of notepaper or interestingly decorated paper.

2. Ask each participant to write a promissory note to himself or herself outlining what he or she intends to do as a result of the learning experience.

3. Encourage participants to be very explicit as to the details of the implementation and the time frame involved.

4. Ask them to address the letter to themselves, seal it, and pass it to the front or use it as a ticket out at the end of the workshop or session.

When

- We want participants to commit to a task.
- We want participants to transfer workshop ideas into the workplace.

- We want to elicit commitment to action.
- We want to remind folks of their commitment at a later date.

Examples and Uses

1. After a workshop on differentiated strategies for middle school students, teachers wrote what and how they were going to implement some of the ideas that they had learned. One participant wrote the following:

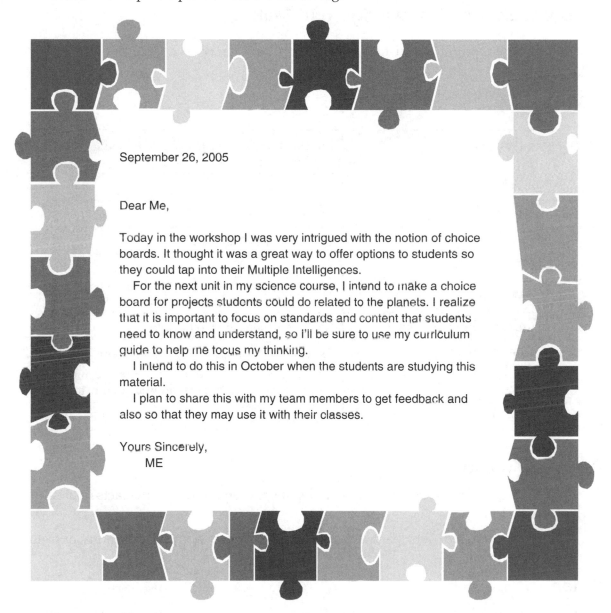

September 26, 2005

Dear Me,

Today in the workshop I was very intrigued with the notion of choice boards. It thought it was a great way to offer options to students so they could tap into their Multiple Intelligences.

For the next unit in my science course, I intend to make a choice board for projects students could do related to the planets. I realize that it is important to focus on standards and content that students need to know and understand, so I'll be sure to use my curriculum guide to help me focus my thinking.

I intend to do this in October when the students are studying this material.

I plan to share this with my team members to get feedback and also so that they may use it with their classes.

Yours Sincerely,
ME

Selected References

Colan (2003), Costa and Garmston (2002), Mind Tools (2006a, 2006b, 2006c), Robbins (1991).

STRATEGY 25

Right Angle

Purpose: Sharing Knowledge and Skills

This is effective as a reflection tool looking at a topic or issue and responding to it at a tangent.

Basics

Number of Participants	May be done individually, in small table group, or as a large group
Time Needed	4–5 minutes
Room Arrangement	Table groups
Difficulty Level	Low risk, easy
Brain Bits	Emotional impact and social support, development of cognitive learning in terms of developing common vocabulary, clarifying, and sharing
Brain's Natural Learning Systems	Emotional, cognitive, reflective
Adult Learning Principle	Experiential: connects to what we know and do well
	Life application: determines real-life use and process of transfer to participants' unique circumstances
Materials	Paper and pen or pencil

Process Directions

1. At the right hand side of the right angle, the participant fills in the facts related to the topic or issue.

2. At the bottom, the participant responds to the issue with opinions, reactions, or feelings.

When

- Participants need to think about an issue from the intuitive sense and react from personal perspective with emotions and opinions.
- We want to know how people think and feel toward a new idea or concept.
- We want to encourage people to share honest reactions to build trust and clarity.

Selected References

Bellanca (1990), Burke (1993), Gregory and Parry (2006), Junior Reserve Officers Training Corps (2006), Murphy (1994), NCREL (2006).

Examples and Uses

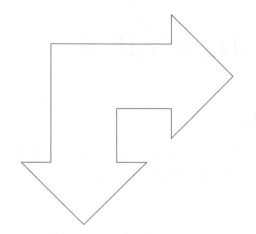

Boys in our school are scoring lower on writing tests than girls.

I think, feel

   That is because many of the boys are developmentally behind girls in the area of language development and also writing is a relatively sedentary activity. Perhaps if we could build more kinesthetic aspects into the writing process, it would be more engaging for boys. Also, I sometimes think the topics could be more appealing to boys.

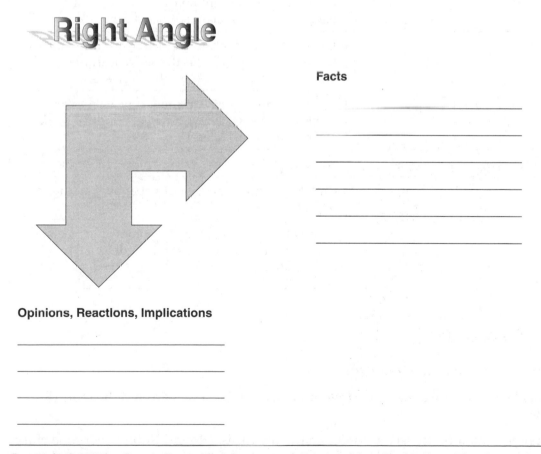

Facts

_____

_____

_____

_____

_____

_____

Opinions, Reactions, Implications

_____

_____

_____

_____

STRATEGY 26

Round Robin, Round Table

Purpose: Sharing Knowledge and Skills

This strategy helps facilitate dialogue, helps process information, is interactive, is inclusive of all participation, helps share knowledge, and helps with problem solving.

Basics

Number of Participants	Groups of three to five
Time Needed	15–20 minutes
Room Arrangement	Table groups or small semicircles near a chart stand or taped up chart paper
Difficulty Level	Easy to begin, momentum carries it forward as participants build on each other's thoughts and ideas
Brain Bits	Emotional and social needs met, helps form patterns to seek meaning, includes the active learning environment that supports adult learning
Adult Learning Principles	Provides opportunities to connect new ideas or actions to what we know, how we prioritize work and determine usefulness
Brain's Natural Learning Systems	Social, emotional, physical, cognitive, reflective
Materials	Chairs, table (optional), chart paper on wall, stand or table, tape, markers
Other	A good team builder at the beginning of a meeting A safe way to brainstorm and include equal participation

Process Directions

1. Each person adds a thought to the topic.

2. It may be written on a piece of paper or poster as it is passed around the table (Round Table).

3. It may be stated orally as a recorder charts the ideas. (Round Robin: everyone chirping up!)

When

- We want to make sure everyone's ideas are heard and included.
- We are brainstorming or reviewing ideas.
- People need multiple points of view prior to decision making or problem solving.
- We want to build commitment through inclusive reception to ideas.

Examples and Uses

1. After a video clip, ask participants one positive thing they saw in the video.

2. Brainstorm ways to get reluctant learners to participate in class discussions.

3. Suggest ways to include technology in the everyday work in the classroom.

4. What is one assessment tool that you used with your students today?

5. You may also begin with a graphic organizer such as the life preserver. Each section is labeled with one aspect for discussion or brainstorming.

6. There may be four people in a group. Person 1 is the first recorder and records ideas for the team in the first section. Person 2 records for the second section and so on.

Selected References

Annenberg Institute for School Reform (1998); Bellanca (1990); Hoffman and Olson-Ness (1996); Kagan (1992); Lipton, Humbard, and Wellman (2001).

Form Base Groups (a)

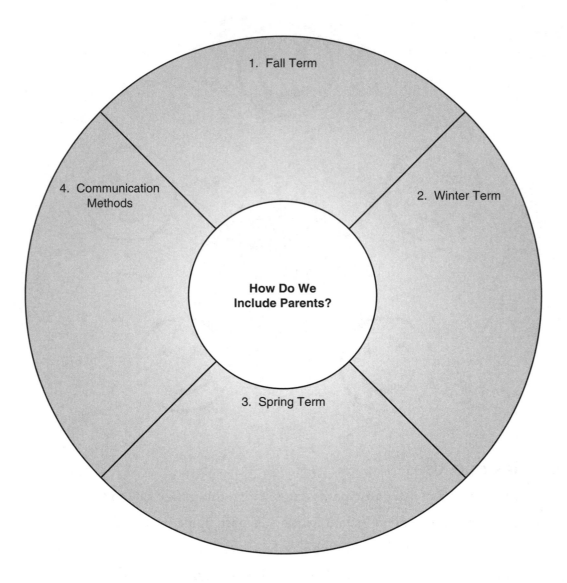

STRATEGY 27

Round the Room Brainstorming

Purpose: Sharing Knowledge and Skills

When trying to generate multiple solutions, people can often use Round the Room Brainstorming. It synergizes the group by showing evidence of the collective power of group problem solving or creative thought. Collectively, folks have more and better ideas than one person working alone.

Basics

Number of Participants	Small groups of five or six working together
	In a very large group, you may need multiple copies of charts on several walls
Time Needed	20–30 minutes including reporting out and debriefing
Room Arrangement	Small groups with a chart for each group
Difficulty Level	Low risk, a little more complex to set up
Brain Bits	Emotional impact and social support, development of cognitive learning in terms of developing common vocabulary, clarifying, and sharing
	Brain loves to solve problems and is resourceful given a challenge
Brain's Natural Learning Systems	Social, emotional, physical, cognitive
Adult Learning Principle	Experiential: connects to what we know and do well
	Life application: determines real-life use and process of transfer to participants' unique circumstances
Materials	Chart paper and markers (masking tape if chart is not self sticking)

Process Directions

1. Divide into groups, one group for each chart.

2. Each group should stand in front of a chart.

3. Choose a scribe in each group. Each group will use a different colored marker. The marker will go with the group from chart to chart. That way, if there are any questions about the suggestion, it's easy to ask the group using that color to clarify their ideas.

4. Quickly brainstorm responses to the topic on the chart.

5. After a minute or two, and when the signal is heard, move one chart to the right.

6. Quickly brainstorm at the new chart (1–2 minutes).

7. At the signal, move to the right and repeat.

8. When you reach the original chart where the group started, analyze the data. Select or prioritize, cluster, or eliminate items.

9. Report out.

10. You may then do a gallery walk to jot down ideas people might want to try.

11. Small groups could take away charts and collate for the group.

12. The planning group could take away the charts and create a plan for the group to peruse at the next meeting.

When

- Participants need some active involvement related to their own well-being.
- People need a change of state and another colleague to discuss an idea.
- People need to move or get up.
- The facilitator needs to lower the risk for participation.
- Dialogue and creating consensus are necessary.
- There is a need for team building.

Examples and Uses

When teachers are implementing new strategies, there are bound to be dips in the road. Challenges and roadblocks that slow down the implementation almost always occur.

1. For example, when using flexible grouping, teachers may find that sometimes when students are working in groups, problems arise. If teachers bring these to the next meeting, they can post their problem on a piece of chart paper.

   It may be "What to do with the student who . . . ?"

2. These problems can be placed at the top of a piece of chart paper for groups to brainstorm suggestions.

Selected References

Annenberg Institute for School Reform (1998), Bellanca (1990), Chang and Dalziel (1999a), Wald and Castleberry (2000).

Doesn't want to work in a group	Takes control

Doesn't participate	Wastes time

1. Have new teachers write a problem they are having on slips of paper. These are placed one on each piece of chart paper, and the group brainstorms suggestions. Not all ideas will work in every case, but it gives a bank of resource suggestions from which the new teacher can select to try and solve his or her problem.

2. Consider Daniel Goleman's Emotional Intelligence domains: Teachers may want to foster the growth of students in each area and do some brainstorming of strategies for each domain. Charts could be labeled with the following
   a. Self-Awareness
   b. Managing Emotions
   c. Self-Motivation
   d. Empathy
   e. Social Skills

1.

2.

3.

4.

5.

STRATEGY 28

Star Gazing

Purpose: Sharing Knowledge and Skills

Groups that share knowledge and skills must respect diversity in experience and contributions from a group. This strategy is great for getting all voices in the room, creating consensus, team building, and an excellent way to see issues or problems from a variety of perspectives. Star Gazing allows us to ask each other key critical questions in order to make the best decisions about teaching and learning, decision making, school issues and other topics that merit sharing our diverse expertise and perspectives.

Basics

Number of Participants	May be done in small table groups or as a large group
Time Needed	10–15 minutes
Room Arrangement	Table groups
Difficulty Level	Low risk, easy
Brain Bits	Emotional impact and social support, development of cognitive learning in terms of developing common vocabulary, clarifying, and sharing
Brain's Natural Learning Systems	Emotional, social, cognitive, reflective
Adult Learning Principle	Experiential: connects to what we know and do well Life application: determines real-life use and process of transfer to participants' unique circumstances
Materials	Chart paper and markers

Process Directions

1. Each person has a copy of the Star and responds to the prompts individually.
2. Then he or she can share with others at his or her table or team in a Round Robin fashion or do a Walk About, in which each person shares each point with a different colleague. A whole-group discussion might ensue after the individual and partner processing.

When

- Participants need some active involvement related to their own well-being.
- People need a change of state and another colleague to discuss an idea.
- People need to move or get up.
- The facilitator needs to lower the risk for participation.
- Dialogue and creating consensus are necessary.
- There is a need for team building.

Examples and Uses

1. Use for discussion of an idea from five different perspectives or points of view.

2. Use the levels of Bloom (1984) to examine a concept.

   Recall or describe
   Compare or contrast
   Associate or connect
   Analyze or take apart
   Synthesize or apply
   Evaluate

3. The points of view relate to a person's thinking about differentiation.

4. This may be used as a focus activity at the beginning or end of a group session.

5. This could be used as a processing piece to generate discussion, create energy during a session, or check for understanding.

Selected References

Bidart (2003), Enchanted Learning (2006a, 2006b), Gregory and Kuzmich (2004).

FIVE POINTS OF VIEW

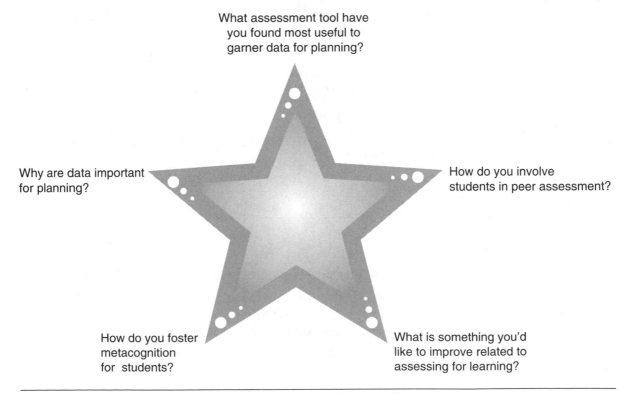

What assessment tool have you found most useful to garner data for planning?

Why are data important for planning?

How do you involve students in peer assessment?

How do you foster metacognition for students?

What is something you'd like to improve related to assessing for learning?

FIVE POINTS OF VIEW

5 Points of View

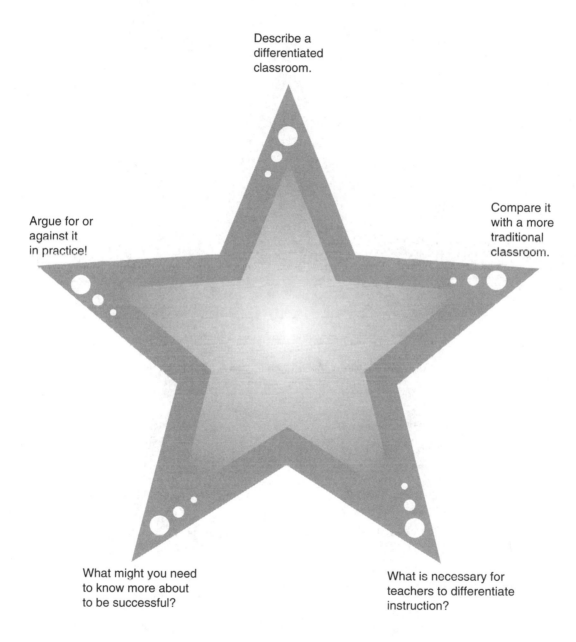

Describe a differentiated classroom.

Compare it with a more traditional classroom.

Argue for or against it in practice!

What might you need to know more about to be successful?

What is necessary for teachers to differentiate instruction?

FIVE POINTS OF VIEW

STRATEGY 29

Think, Pair, Share

Purpose: Sharing Knowledge and Skills

Think, Pair, Share is a strategy that increases the time for thinking so that the brain does not "downshift" to the fight and flight response. This strategy facilitates wait time that Mary Budd Rowe (1987) suggested was necessary to receive quality answers from students. Think, Pair, Share allows time for talk about the topic or concept and increases the quality of thinking and the responses that ensue.

Basics

Number of Participants	Partners
Time Needed	5 minutes
Room Arrangement	Tables, rows standing
Difficulty Level	Low risk, easy
Brain Bits	Emotional impact and social support, development of cognitive learning in terms of developing common vocabulary, clarifying, and sharing
Brain's Natural Learning Systems	Social, emotional, cognitive, physical, reflective
Adult Learning Principle	Experiential: connects to what we know and do well Life application: determines real-life use and process of transfer to participants' unique circumstances
Materials	None

Process Directions

1. A question or idea is presented.

2. The prompt might be to think about the question or idea that is presented.

3. Give about 30 seconds for people to think.

4. Say, "Now turn to a partner and share your answer."

5. Pairs discuss for 60 seconds and then are asked to share with the whole group.

When

- Participants need some active involvement related to their own well-being.
- People need a change of state and another colleague to discuss an idea.

- People need to move or get up.
- The facilitator needs to lower the risk for participation.
- Dialogue and creating consensus are necessary.
- There is a need for team building.

Selected References

Johnson, Johnson, and Smith (1991a, 1991b); Johnson and Johnson (1994); Kagan (1992); Lyman (1981); Lyman and McTighe (2001).

Examples and Uses

1. Describe a way you differentiate in your classroom.

2. How would you help a new student assimilate into the class?

3. What graphic organizer are you using most often?

4. From your perspective, what is the biggest priority for this team?

STRATEGY 30

Wallpaper Poster

Purpose: Sharing Knowledge and Skills

To attend to more learning styles, we need to go beyond verbal linguistic to visual spatial. We also want to summarize and clearly state information in precise ways.

Basics

Number of Participants	May be done in small table groups or as partners
Time Needed	10–15 minutes or longer depending on the content
Room Arrangement	Table groups
Difficulty Level	Low risk, easy
Brain Bits	Emotional impact and social support, development of cognitive learning in terms of developing common vocabulary, clarifying, and sharing
Brain's Natural Learning System	Social, cognitive, physical, reflective
Adult Learning Principle	Experiential: connects to what we know and do well Life application: determines real-life use and process of transfer to participants' unique circumstances
Materials	Chart paper and markers

Process Directions

1. Have participants read an article or perhaps view a video noting the key points. You could ask different groups to attend to different topics.

2. Have partners or small groups place the topic on the top of a piece of chart paper.

3. Next, people will define the concept in their own words.

4. Then, create a symbol to represent the concept visually.

5. Next, give examples that support the idea and be able to rationalize them.

6. Present to another small group or entire group.

When

- Participants need some active involvement related to their own well-being as well as to develop a deeper understanding of a concept or new idea.
- People need a change of state and another colleague to discuss an idea.
- People need to move or get up.
- The facilitator needs to lower the risk for participation.
- Dialogue and creating consensus are necessary.

Examples and Uses

1. Teachers will take an assessment tool by pulling a paper from the fishbowl. They will research the strategy and create a wallpaper poster.

2. Teachers will take one of the Multiple Intelligences at random, investigate it, and create a wallpaper task to express their understanding of it.

3. Teachers will view a video about differentiated instructional strategies, select one, and prepare a wallpaper task.

Selected References

Beaudoin and Taylor (2004); Chang and Dalziel (1999a); Erickson (2005); Gregory, Robbins, and Herndon (2000); Hoffman and Olson-Ness (1996); Marzano (2004); Taba (1967); Wald and Castleberry (2000).

Wallpaper Poster

Record the title on the top of the chart paper.

1. Define the concept (key ideas).

2. Design a symbol for the concept.

3. Give examples for the concept. Be prepared to state your rationale for selection.

CHAPTER

3

Building Resilience and Creating Solutions

Sustaining any profound change process requires a fundamental shift in thinking. We need to understand the nature of growth processes (forces that aid our efforts) and how to catalyze them. But we also need to understand the forces and challenges that impede progress, and to develop workable strategies for dealing with these challenges.

—Peter Senge et al. (1999, p. 10)

STARTING VERSUS SUSTAINING

It is one thing to get groups of professionals together and learn strategy, read a book, or have some meaningful discussions. It is another challenge altogether to sustain such learning communities over time and work to create solutions that have a true impact on results for students. Sustainable results are the ultimate goal for such learning communities. We all want student achievement that can be replicated regardless of conditions and personnel. Groups that evolve over time are ready to take on different challenges. Sometimes groups get stuck and need strategies that help them move forward. Sometimes groups try solutions, but get frustrated with lack of results or slow results. At these times, groups need strategies that create renewal, overcome resistance to change, and focus on solutions. Daryl Conner (1998) in his book, *Leading at the Edge of Chaos*, writes about change and how teams sometimes come to the edge of chaos. He notes that especially at this vulnerable point for a group of professionals, creating opportunity out of that experience rather than stagnation is essential. Conner also reminds us of the need to keep challenge and capability in mind. If challenge exceeds capability, we feel overwhelmed; but if capability exceeds challenge, we feel energized (Covey, 1989). Our purpose in presenting these strategies is to help you create that opportunity for energizing and sustaining your forward momentum. Such strategies will help you form the basis of capable teams whose energy benefits our students.

BUILDING RESILIENCE

Rosabeth Kanter (1984) in her book, *Change Masters*, notes that people resist change for very good reasons. Many of our strategies in this book help support the actions that build resilience.

Building Resilience		
Worries	*Actions That Cause Resistance*	*Actions That Build Resilience*
Loss of Control	Change is exciting when it done by us, threatening when it is done to us.	• Involve people in the earliest aspects of change. • Make certain people have choice. • Share decision making.
Excess Uncertainty	If we don't know where the next step will lead, we tend to stay put.	• Make risk taking safe even if the results aren't always predictable. • Communicate early and often. • Provide organization and structure. • Set personal goals to decide first steps.
Surprise	We tend to resist that for which we have had no time to prepare.	• Give plenty of lead time where possible; if it is not possible then say why, and communicate early and often. • Invite predictions. • Build resilience.

Building Resilience		
Worries	Actions That Cause Resistance	Actions That Build Resilience
Lack of the Familiar	Our desire for familiar surroundings is strong. Change threatens us as we are forced to alter routines and habits.	• Make connections to what is known. • Honor past accomplishments. • Stress the purpose for change. • Provide structure for discussions. • Allow choice in how to proceed with change.
Loss of Face	Loss of face means having to admit that the way things were done in the past was wrong or at least not the best way.	• Work off of successes and not gaps. What actions made something positive happen? Could we apply those same actions to tackle new problems? This is called asset mapping. • Create blame-free zones through norm setting and monitoring the risk level.
Doubts About Competence	We become concerned about our competence. Will I make it under the new circumstances? Do I have the skills to compete or contribute in the new situation?	• Foster an attitude of "We are all in this together." • Create a sense that if everyone is a learner, no one is expected to have the changes perfected yet. • Teams that create an "ongoing learner" perspective overcome this worry.
Disruption of Personal Life	Change often disrupts personal time or needs.	• Manage and respect time in a team. • Careful pre-planning makes the time worthwhile. • Divide the work into manageable chunks with regard to load and time.
Perception of "More Work"	The effort to manage one's affairs is multiplied when things are changed.	• Even if we are doing things "smarter and not harder" or replacing old strategies with new, we need to help each other with the little "how to's" that make new things work better quicker. • Be explicit in describing which strategies or actions we are replacing or substituting. • Help each other with the logistics as well as the big ideas.

(Continued)

(Continued)

Building Resilience		
Worries	*Actions That Cause Resistance*	*Actions That Build Resilience*
Past Resentments	Unresolved issues from the past rise up to entangle and hamper the change effort.	• "Journey Mapping," "Environmental Scanning," and other strategies for teams that get people to "park the junk" work well. • We need to acknowledge what occurred without letting it slow us down now. • Facilitate carefully so that individuals' points of view are respected, yet do not derail the team's forward movement.
Worry That There Will Be Winners and Losers	Sometimes change does create "winners and losers" or "haves and have-nots."	• Resources get distributed differently in times of change. • Good decision-making practices that focus on a "win-win" orientation keep this worry at bay. • Decide ahead of time how conflict and problems will be resolved; establish a well-communicated process.

This chart is adapted from the works of Kanter, Kuzmich, Gregory, and Parry.

We have noted that if our teams, work groups, or professional learning communities control for these factors and utilize the right strategies, we can build resilience rather than cause resistance. The strategies in this chapter were carefully selected to help teams deal with the high degree of change that currently characterizes learning organizations.

MOTIVATION

Every meaningful change effort results in implementation dips somewhere along the way, and self-motivation needs to be high to make it through these tougher times. As we begin implementation, we have energy and enthusiasm. However, as we hit bumps in the road, we don't progress as quickly as expected, we encounter problems, or challenges surface, teams sometimes become discouraged or simply tired. At these times, we need the team to problem solve and encourage one another to stay focused on success. A group, like an individual, lives up to expectations set forth in its surroundings. The higher the expectations of a group for a successful result, the greater the probability that a positive goal will be reached. It's the notion of self-motivation and the ability to delay gratification with the hope of success while persisting toward the goal that makes a group achieve success. There are strategies that build a group's resilience and foster motivation. Such strategies help individuals and groups engage in meaningful work. Several of the strategies help establish positive relationships and connections. We know from brain research and psychological studies that individuals within groups stay more motivated if the actions and activities of the group are meaningful and result in a sense of worth and accomplishment. These positive emotions fuel the work of the group over time in a powerful way.

CREATIVE SOLUTIONS

A high-performing team that get results has certain characteristics; one of these is the ability to sustain and cultivate creative problem solving. In his book, *A Whole New Mind,* Daniel Pink (2005) talks about six senses that will help people be successful in this new global age. These senses are required for groups that want to navigate rapid change with resilience and creativity.

Pink (2005) talks about the ability to

- Creatively design,
- Tell the story,
- Create symphony (put all the pieces together),
- Show empathy,
- Play (humor and group fun helps creativity), and
- Establish meaning or purpose. (pp. 65–66)

Individuals who demonstrate these "senses" are more likely to be successful in our changing world. Groups that can emulate that creative spirit will generate amazing solutions with and for our students. Several of the strategies in this book are designed to help groups develop creative solutions and demonstrate those characteristics of high-performing teams.

GOT SUCCESS?

Lee Colan says that "success does not depend upon the brilliance of your plan, but upon the consistency of your actions" (2003, p. 3). He goes on to describe the need for successful teams to get more focused and structured when they go through difficult times. Educators are passionate about the success of students. During certain times, teams need to re-energize by focusing on this passion for our work. Balancing the work, creating clarity in the target we are after, and structuring the work helps us build resilience and solve problems. When teams emerge from this phase, they are ready to create powerful solutions and change.

PRIMARY PURPOSE FOR THE STRATEGIES IN THIS SECTION

In this chapter, we offer you strategies to determine priorities and create excellence:

- Sustaining momentum
- Solving problems
- Unsticking teams
- Managing change
- Developing creative solutions to challenges

STRATEGY 31

DIP Party

Purpose: Building Resilience and Creating Solutions

A DIP Party is a fun way to celebrate accomplishments along the way, share new knowledge, and re-energize for the next task. This is a great way to build resilience.

Basics

Number of Participants	Any size school-based or district-based team
Time Needed	30 minutes
Room Arrangement	Tables and chairs
Difficulty Level	Low risk, easy
Brain Bits	Emotional impact and social support, development of cognitive learning in terms of developing common vocabulary, an interactive activity re-energizes
Adult Learning Principle	Experiential: connects to what we know and do well Life application: determines real-life use and process of transfer to participants' unique circumstances
Materials	Food, chart paper, and markers
Other	If the recipe card activity does not fit your team, you could use other methods. Several processing methods would work with this concept including SWOT, Cause and Effect, Roadblocks

Process Directions

1. Use when staff has a dip in morale, as a celebration, or when work is at a standstill.

2. Hold a DIP Party. Have people sign up to bring a variety of dips, chips, and vegetables. Use the party invitation to celebrate steps already taken, work accomplished, or initial results.

3. At the party, enjoy the treats and use a processing method that acknowledges what we have accomplished and what we need to do next. What to do next might include removing roadblocks, prioritizing, listing next steps, or determining what we have

control over and what we do not. Use the recipe card template. This can be modified to meet your particular challenges and needs. Other methods listed previously would work as well.

4. If desired, follow-up with a big thank-you note to staff or the team for the work done and an advance thanks for the work coming up. Share both dip recipes and recipes for success if you wish.

When

- Staff are worn out and need a boost.
- A team or staff members are bringing up all the reasons why something cannot get done.
- Progress has been made on a difficult or complex task.
- The group needs to re-energize, reprioritize, and re-establish the target for a group.
- The group needs to celebrate new knowledge and information.

Examples and Uses

1. Staff finishes a fall writing assessment and a review of the data.

2. Fifty new students have registered, and the student mobility has teachers worried.

3. Requirements for assessment changed yet again, and staff seem less resilient.

4. A team takes on problem-based math and partway through realizes how much background knowledge students need to be successful. Celebration along the way makes the hard work more positive.

5. Staff are trying to work on multiple projects such as implementing reading comprehension strategies, writing strategies, discipline processes, and content area adoptions all at the same time.

6. Staff need an occasion to celebrate, given the implementation of new strategies or new knowledge.

Selected Reference

Gregory (2005).

Some Recipe Cards for the DIP Party

Lin Kuzmich's Favorite DIP: Onion and Dill Weed Dip

Mix:

1 cup sour cream

1 cup mayonnaise

1 tablespoon Worchester

1 tablespoon chopped parsley

1 teaspoon dill weed

1 tablespoon minced onion

½ teaspoon pepper

¼ teaspoon salt

1 teaspoon Beau Monde

Then refrigerate for one hour. Stir before serving. Serve with chips or vegetables.

Gayle Gregory's Favorite DIP: Hot Artichoke Dip

Mix:

4 oz. bottle pimento, chopped

4 oz. can artichoke hearts, drained and chopped

4 oz. cheddar cheese, grated

1 ½ cup mayonnaise

1½ cup Parmesan cheese

3 drops of hot sauce

Place in deep 1½-quart baking dish. Sprinkle with a little extra cheese and pimento. Bake in a conventional oven at 325 degrees for 30 minutes or microwave on high for 10 minutes until bubbly. Serve with corn chips, tortilla chips, or pita.

Processing Card for DIP Party Activity

Recipe for Success
List next steps we need to take.
What we will celebrate next.
What roadblocks should we remove and how?
How will we encourage and support each other?

Other Food-Oriented Ideas for Renewal and Refocus

Soup party in the middle of winter

Cookie-fest right before state testing

Chili cook-off

STRATEGY 32

Checking the Oil

Purpose: Building Resilience and Creating Solutions

This strategy is a great method for passing on the hard work of the previous years to the new staff. It helps to capture and celebrate accomplishments for existing staff. "Checking the Oil" also sustains resilience in buildings and on teams.

Basics

Number of Participants	Small teams, departments, or whole staff
Time Needed	Time varies with who does what and the elaborateness of the artifacts. In its simplest form, could be done in 20–30 minutes
Room Arrangement	Any arrangement of tables and chairs
Difficulty Level	Easy and lower risk
Brain Bits	Adults love connections and patterns; a historical perspective helps connect the old with the new
Adult Learning Principle	Passing on expertise is a part of making the work life applicable and honors the experiences gathered over time
Materials	Charts and markers, template to start the process
Other	Can be done with actual artifacts, photos, articles, student work, plans, and so forth

Process Directions

1. Introduce new staff and explain the task of catching the new folks up with all our hard work.

2. Split staff into four groups and have them describe the work we have done in the last three to five years in the following:
   a. Standards, assessment, and alignment
   b. Knowing our students
   c. Best practices and strategies
   d. Articles, books, or videos that really helped us learn

3. Each group shares its list with the whole staff.

4. Optional step: Divide up to put together a notebook—sort of a manual for the excellent instruction in this building (just like a car manual) for each new teacher, and maybe for everyone, that contains "the best of...," so that all this knowledge and some

samples are included. Notebooks could be customized to each content or grade level. This could be done in spring after brainstorming or in the fall after brainstorming as an introduction.

When

- Use when catching up new staff with what we have accomplished in our professional learning community, department, grade level, school, or district team.
- Use when celebrating what we have accomplished in the last few years.
- Use when developing common vocabulary to describe what we regard as essential on this team or in this school for excellent instruction and learning.

Examples and Uses

1. A number of new staff members from various grades and content areas are arriving.

2. Three years of work in writing needs to be recapped before going on to a new project. We want to continue what is successful as we move forward in another area.

3. Each staff member has a variable number of years with our team or school, and not everyone had the same professional development.

4. A new principal or teacher leader takes over a group. Going through this process, honors what has gone on before and orients the new leader.

Selected References

Bailey (1995), Chadwick (2006), Chang and Dalziel (1999b), Deal and Peterson (1998), Gregory and Kuzmich (2004), Jones (2005), Roberts and Pruitt (2003), Wald and Castleberry (2000).

CHANGING THE OIL

Directions

Please brainstorm a list of where we focused our energy and resources in the last three years.

Standards, Assessment, and Alignment	**Knowing Our Students**
Best Practices and Strategies	**Articles, Books, Training, or Media That Have Influenced Our Work**

STRATEGY 33

Communication Matters

Purpose: Building Resilience and Creating Solutions

It is vitally important to professional learning teams of any size to develop, agree upon, and use communication methods that will be respectful of and useful to the group. This method is a way to set all the professional learning communities (PLCs) in a building on a positive track.

Basics

Number of Participants	Any number
Time Needed	20–30 minutes for initial solution development, follow-up includes getting the choices out to professional learning communities or stakeholders (moments if by e-mail), deciding which to use (10 minutes) and follow-up check-in (5–10 minutes)
Room Arrangement	Small groups to create choice board for communication
Difficulty Level	Moderate, requires participants to honestly reflect on how they will access information and then commit to using those methods regularly
Brain Bits	Social connections are essential to adult learning, and information keeps the flow of ideas moving forward
Adult Learning Principle	Adults like to be kept informed and seek not to be surprised by upcoming issues and actions; adults need to connect what they are doing and to reflect real-life application
Materials	Template and markers
Other	This process could be used, with the same chart, for staff information and parent-group communication

Process Directions

1. Introduce the idea of customizing communication methods and choice in using those methods.

2. Get each small table group to brainstorm a list of communication methods that would work well for multiple purposes, staff information, PLC interactions and meeting agendas, and so forth.

3. Get a small representative group to summarize the work and create one Communication Choice Board for the school.

4. Then, at the next PLC meeting, each PLC picks up to three methods of communication off the choice board.

5. Follow-up is recommended to check whether the methods chosen are useful and used by all participants.

When

- Use at the start of the school year.
- Use at the start of a specific group's work.
- Use for planning for the following year or at a particularly hectic time of the year.

Examples and Uses

1. Use for starting a specific-purpose group such as a Parent/Teacher Association, an advisory committee, a prom committee, literacy teams, or departments, or as updates to various groups, and so forth.

2. Use when PLCs are formed.

3. Use for getting updates on school issues during state assessment schedule changes.

4. Use when setting up a regular cycle of communication for the school's shared decision-making group so that everyone else knows what is discussed, decided, or at issue.

Selected References

Gregory and Kuzmich (2005a, 2005b), Tomlinson (2001).

COMMUNICATION MATTERS

An Example of a Communication Choice Board

Prior Preparation: Brainstorm methods of communication that would work across groups and purposes for the groups. A small representative committee would put this together for everyone to use.

E-mail update sent out every _____ by _____ _____ _____	Group (or individual) newsletter created every _____ by _____ _____ _____ _____	Graffiti board or other posting located _____ _____ _____ _____
Web site posting updated every _____ by _____ _____ _____	FREE CHOICE A unique method that suits your group: _____ _____ _____ _____ _____	Bulletin board that everyone checks every _____ _____ _____ _____ _____
Mailbox memo checked every _____ _____ _____ _____ _____	Text messaging every _____ _____ _____ _____ _____	List on shared "blog" (web log or journal) and checked every _____ _____ _____ _____

STRATEGY 34

Doubling Up

Purpose: Building Resilience and Creating Solutions

This method is a process that honors multiple resources and levels of expertise in groups. It is always helpful to compare points of view and share processing.

Basics

Number of Participants	4 to 400
Time Needed	First pairing 4 minutes, second pairing 8 minutes, and third pairing 16 minutes
Room Arrangement	Floor space to move from pairing to pairing
Difficulty Level	Very easy
Brain Bits	Adults love movement and social interaction to further their learning; problem solving with others and sampling perspectives is also part of brain-friendly adult learning
Adult Learning Principle	Adults like and need the opportunity to hear points of view and relate them to applications in their own world; adults also like strategies and solutions that they are comfortable trying; comfort level is increased when valued peers have already successfully tried something new
Materials	Note-taking tools
Other	Great sharing for parent groups as well

Process Directions

1. Give a prompt to think about and ask each individual to write down one or more ideas, solutions, or strategies in response to the prompt.
2. Share your responses with a partner.
3. In the second round, you and your partner find another pair and share discussion or aha moments.
4. In the third round, the four of you seek out another four. Share what you have listed quickly and then brainstorm a few more to add to your list of solutions, strategies, and ideas.

When

- Great for creative problem solving
- Wonderful way to get unstuck on an issue or problem
- Great way to come to consensus on decision making

Examples and Uses

1. How are you implementing the new writing strategies?
2. Use for decision making around budget priorities for next year.
3. The is good for creating ideas and strategies for managing a differentiated classroom.
4. Resources for great math problems, social studies supplemental materials, science experiments, and so forth can be collected.

Selected References

Johnson and Johnson (1994); Johnson, Johnson, and Smith (1991a, 1991b); Kagan (1992); Lyman and McTighe (2001).

DOUBLING UP

Ways to Set Up Partners and Sharing

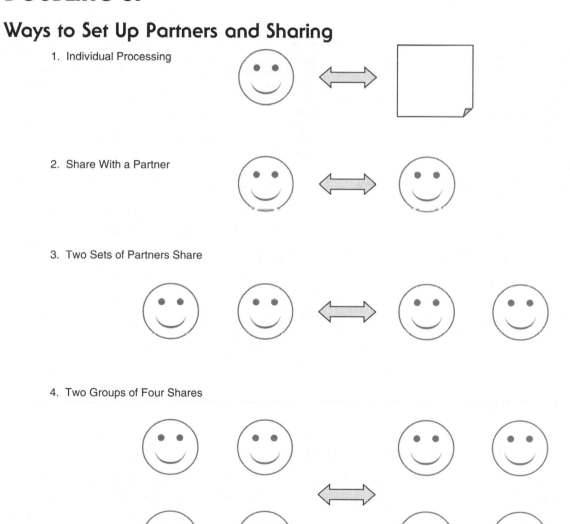

1. Individual Processing

2. Share With a Partner

3. Two Sets of Partners Share

4. Two Groups of Four Shares

STRATEGY 35

Environmental Scanning

Purpose: Building Resilience and Creating Solutions

It is critical to the health of groups to take stock of the influences and stressors on that group and then to decide what to do about them. There are both internal and external sources of stress that impact any group. Identifying these and deciding what can and cannot be done to mitigate these influences is important to moving forward.

Basics

Number of Participants	Small group or groups of four to eight
Time Needed	60 minutes
Room Arrangement	Small groups at tables
Difficulty Level	Moderate since some of the topics discussed can be controversial
Brain Bits	Understanding social and emotional pressures helps a group function and development more effective interactive strategies over time; this method also supports the reflective learning needs of adults
Adult Learning Principle	Adults need opportunities to prioritize work, reflect, and orient, and they have a high need for real-life application
Materials	Chart paper, markers, and tape
Other	Works well with "Target Practice" or other priority-setting strategies as a follow-up

Process Directions

1. Explain the need to define the pressures and influences on our group for us to be aware of what is occurring and to plan accordingly.

2. Brainstorm with the total group all of the external and internal influences or sources of pressure and stress on the group. (You could also come with pre-prepared areas. See examples.)

3. Quickly group these items. Split participants or teams into groups with charts labeled for the area of pressure or stress.

4. Have smaller groups brainstorm why these areas might be sources of stress or pressure.

5. Record and select a reporter and hang up the chart.

6. Report on the findings of each group.

7. Invite the total group to add anything to each list (general feedback, or use a Gallery Walk).

8. Facilitate a discussion of how this scan of the environment can help us plan for the future.

When

- Use when groups get stuck or frustrated.
- Use at the start or end of the year.
- Use when rapid changes are coming at a group.

Examples and Uses

1. Federal requirements change—again.

2. State requirements change—again.

3. The district has mandated a different format, method, materials, or process for getting work done or holding people accountable. For example, if there is a new way of recording the work of professional learning teams, or an action planning process changes with a new Board of Education or superintendent.

4. Leaders notice that teams feel stressed or overworked, feel that they have too much "on the plate," or when pressure to increase performance is heightened.

Selected References

Alberta Department of Education (2002), Bailey (1990), Destra Consulting Group (2002), National School Board Association (2005).

ENVIRONMENTAL SCANNING

Environmental Scanning

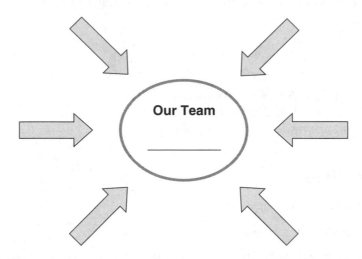

If you want to skip the brainstorming step and pre-prepare topics for the small groups to consider, try these or other concerns:

External Forces

- Federal legislation
- State legislation
- Graduation requirements at the state level
- Resources allocated by federal or state agencies
- Governmental assessment
- Service requirements for various subgroups
- Political agendas
- Parental pressures
- Technology

Internal Forces

- District policies
- Graduation requirements
- District assessment requirements
- District or school professional development requirements
- Resource allocation and access
- Staff issues
- Leadership initiatives at the district level
- Time
- Organizational goals and objectives, strategic plans
- Technology
- Departmental or grade-level issues

STRATEGY 36

FLOW

Purpose: Building Resilience and Creating Solutions

This is a method of brainstorming that helps participants increase creativity and solution orientation.

Basics

Number of Participants	Any number
Time Needed	10 minutes
Room Arrangement	Small or large groups
Difficulty Level	Very easy
Brain Bits	The brain stores information in networks that are associated; certain methods of brainstorming help activate those natural connections and associations that lead to creative thinking
Adult Learning Principle	Adults need choice and seek creativity when relevance to their own situation is high
Materials	Chart paper and markers
Other	None

Process Directions

1. Review directions for brainstorming activity using FLOW rules.

2. Conduct the brainstorming on any given topic by having individuals write down a few ideas first and then take turns sharing.

3. Review how well FLOW rules helped the participants, and remind people that connecting with each other's ideas is a good thing to do.

4. Conduct brainstorming for a limited amount of time, and stop before folks start evaluating the ideas.

5. Process the brainstorming without judgment, type up ideas, and send them out to participants for further reflection before the next meeting.

When

- A goal has been set and solutions or action plans need to be developed.
- Data review has taken place and it is time to develop ideas for further results.
- A particular problem has come up due to a change in population or requirements or edicts, and solutions need to be developed.

Examples and Uses

1. This activity is good when solutions for low reading and writing scores among culturally diverse students are needed.

2. The district develops a new process for evaluating success in thinking skills or math and solutions, and creative approaches are necessary.

3. The school has a goal to increase the graduation rate among mobile students, and methods of keeping students in school are needed.

Selected Resources

Gregory (2005).

FLOW Rules for Brainstorming

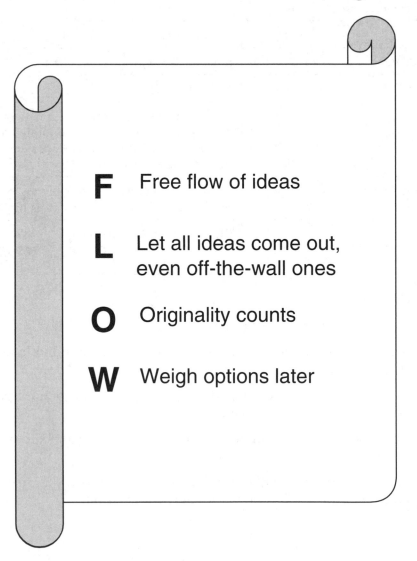

F Free flow of ideas

L Let all ideas come out, even off-the-wall ones

O Originality counts

W Weigh options later

STRATEGY 37

Force Field

Purpose: Building Resilience and Creating Solutions

This process works well when planning major changes and when those changes require coordination. This method also helps when there is a need to value multiple points of view. Avoiding resistance or addressing it early in a project is essential to a successful result. This process directly addresses such resistance and helps staff remove roadblocks to success early in the process of change.

Basics

Number of Participants	Small groups of 5 to 7 or a larger group of up to 50
Time Needed	45–60 minutes
Room Arrangement	Tables and chairs for small groups and large groups
Difficulty Level	This activity is of moderate difficulty; the facilitator needs to keep the participants on task and limit or prohibit any blame placing
Brain Bits	Adults need to learn in trustworthy environments with high expectations and adequate support and structure
Adult Learning Principle	Adults need to connect prior knowledge; adults need choice and opportunities to reflect
Materials	Chart paper and markers or template
Other	This process works well for small learning communities and for larger staff sessions

Process Directions

1. Identify the area for change.

2. Participants, working in partners, write a statement that describes the current state or situation regarding this area or issue.

3. Table groups share the work of the partners. Facilitator asks for descriptions of current state.

4. Table groups or small groups work to develop a list of descriptors for the desired result or change. What do we want instead of the current condition we described?

5. The facilitator makes a list of those descriptors and posts them next to the descriptions of the current state.

6. Small groups now work on a two-part template. What forces are hindering our ability to move to that desired state or result? What forces help us move toward change?

7. Describe ways to overcome the hindrances and support the helping factors.

8. Share as a total group.

9. The final step is to put names, times, and resources next to solutions and set a time to check if the removal of hindrances and support of positive factors is working.

When

- Use prior to a change taking place.
- Use after a new project starts, to check progress.
- Use when any resistance to the change is noted.
- Use at the end of a year when planning the second phase of a multiyear project.

Examples and Uses

1. When initiating a new problem-based math curriculum, resistance may be felt from staff or parents.

2. Use for checking the progress of a new method of conducting searches at the high school.

3. Use when checking progress on a new method of discipline at recess at the elementary level.

4. Use when PLCs are struggling with reading and writing across content areas.

5. Use when the number of non-English speakers has increased dramatically, and staff are trying to figure out strategies for learning and teaching.

Selected References

Chang and Buster (1999), Daniels (1986), Kassouf (1970), Mind Tools (2006a, 2006b, 2006c).

FORCE FIELD

Issue, Topic, or Area of Change

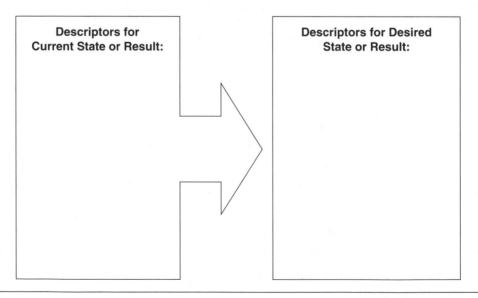

FORCE FIELD: PART TWO

Desired Result

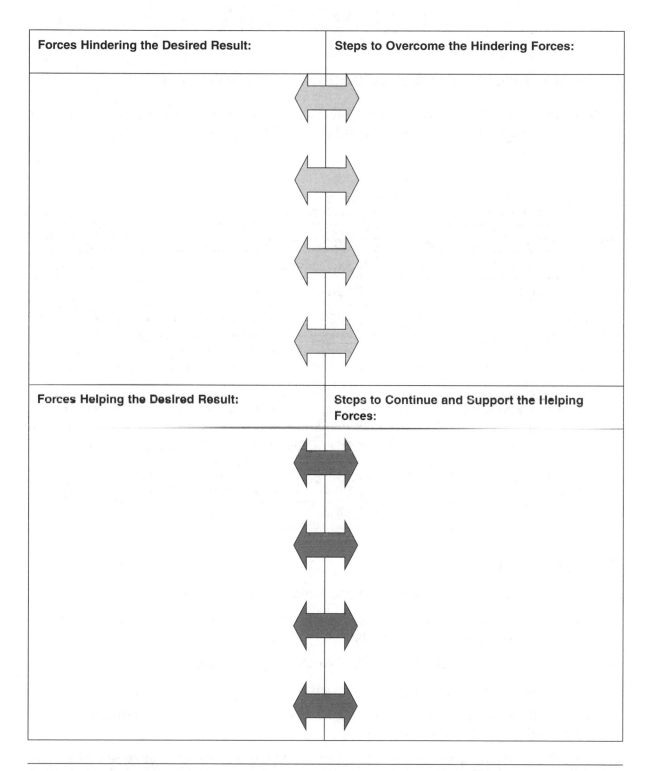

Forces Hindering the Desired Result:	Steps to Overcome the Hindering Forces:
Forces Helping the Desired Result:	**Steps to Continue and Support the Helping Forces:**

STRATEGY 38

Gallery Walk

Purpose: Building Resilience and Creating Solutions

Gallery Walk is a collaborative problem-solving tool. It is an excellent means for communication that acknowledges the creativity and power of the group.

Basics

Number of Participants	Any number
Time Needed	30–45 minutes
Room Arrangement	Small groups
Difficulty Level	Easy two-step process
Brain Bits	Support the adult desire for creativity to be acknowledged, workload to be shared, and connections and patterns to be formed; emotional and social support by the group is also an important part of a healthy work environment
Adult Learning Principle	Adults need to connect new ideas to what they know and do well; adults love choice
	In addition, adults need learning that is immediately applicable to their unique circumstances
Materials	Chart or poster paper, markers and tape
Other	None

Process Directions

1. Introduce this problem-solving method and give an example.

2. Have each small table group select a problem or question to address given the particular topic or area under discussion.

3. Have each group brainstorm a list of solutions and strategies.

4. Then have the groups hang up their charts.

5. Invite the total group to walk around the room and view each chart with a marker and something on which to take notes.

6. Each participant is encouraged to either add to the current list of suggestions or write down some of the ideas he or she finds personally useful.

7. Two wrap-up suggestions: The original small group reviews the additional ideas regarding their issue or problem or processes with the whole group some of the personally useful ideas.

When

- The group is starting work on a goal or has begun work and hit some snags.
- Celebrating the power of the ideas in a group is a great way to sustain resilience.
- The group needs a problem-solving and creativity tool to address problems or issues that have multiple variables or steps.

Examples and Uses

1. Work starts on an action plan around student writing. Staff are able to collect data and analyze needs but may be uncertain as to the best strategies to address those needs. Example: One third of my students need help with voice and sentence structure, and of those students, 75% are English-Language Learners (ELLs). What are the best strategies I could use that address these traits *and* the needs of ELL students?

2. PLCs at a school each took a slightly different approach to solving reading comprehension problems across content areas. Each learning community lists its method or sources and great ideas from this source. Others add good ideas that might help this team go even further.

3. Thorough data collection around attendance has taken place, including interviews of students and parents, surveys, and so forth. Reasons for absences are placed on each chart. Small groups brainstorm solutions, and then others add ideas.

Selected References

Annenberg Institute for School Reform (1998), Chang and Dalziel (1999a), Gibbs (2001), Osborn (1963), Texas Department of Education (2006).

GALLERY WALK: AN EXAMPLE

Problem:

Students are not performing as well as expected on numeracy skills across subgroups in math.

Small-Group Solutions and Strategies:

1. Use research-based methods of acquiring math vocabulary.

2. Use concept formation and Keyword Method.

3. Graphic organizers help students understand thinking about numeracy concepts.

4. Use "manipulatives" to develop concepts.

5. Ask students to state why two or more strategies in math work well and what big ideas work with multiple strategies.

6. Ask students to develop problems to show they understand numeracy ideas.

Additional Ideas From Other Staff Members:

The Frayer Method is a great way to introduce and build upon math concepts.

Include assessment of numeracy concepts in all your formative and summative data-collection tools.

Ask students to detect errors in problems and explain so that you know their correct or faulty assumptions in numeracy.

STRATEGY 39

Graffiti Board

Purpose: Building Resilience and Creating Solutions

Graffiti is a collaborative problem-solving tool. It is excellent for communication that acknowledges the creativity and power of the group.

Basics

Number of Participants	Any number
Time Needed	5 minutes to introduce the concept, 10 minutes to practice, and then can be used by individuals taking only a minute or two every so often
Room Arrangement	Any (small groups for introduction)
Difficulty Level	Easy
Brain Bits	Support the adult desire for creativity to be acknowledged, workload to be shared, and connections and patterns formed; emotional and social support by the group is also an important part of a healthy work environment
Adult Learning Principle	Experiential: Connecting new ideas to what we know and do well
	Self-directed: Adults love choice
	Life applicable: Adults need learning that is immediately applicable to their unique circumstances
Materials	Chart or poster paper, markers, and tape
Other	Designed for problem solving, this method can be used whenever an individual or team wants the perspectives, skills, or solutions of other staff members

Process Directions

1. Introduce this method as a great way to gather ideas from colleagues around problems and issues.

2. Offer a model by putting a topic or problem in the center of a large piece of chart or poster paper. Ask the group to call out solutions, strategies, or points of view. Record those ideas.

3. Process by asking the small groups to discuss ways this method might help them expand their repertoire by connecting with the ideas and perspectives of others.

4. Have each small group come up with one problem or issue. Record it in the center. Ask one person in the small group to record ideas from participants.

5. After hanging these up, offer participants time to look at the work of other groups. (You could combine this with "Round the Room Brainstorming" or "Gallery Walk.")

6. Process how this might help professional learning teams, departments, and grade levels with problem solving.
   a. Suggest that a team try this method by posting a blank chart or poster near where the team gathers or works.
   b. Post a problem, topic, or challenge that is pressing, and ask the team to add solutions, ideas, and strategies to the poster or chart between now and the next time they meet.
   c. Process the answers at the team meeting or learning session.
   d. Try this method of helping each other over the course of the next month or some other agreed-upon time period.

When

- Use for initiating a team or PLC.
- Use for updating methods of communication and sharing.
- Use to add variety to get issues unstuck or moving forward.
- Use to add to the processing strategies of teams, departments, and schools.

Examples and Uses

1. Staff members may have difficulty with student issues such as discipline, mobility, special needs, and attendance.

2. A PLC is focused on certain literacy strategies. The strategy is at the center of the Graffiti Board, and members add ideas for implementation and successful uses as they try the new method.

3. New teachers can get questions answered quickly and easily by putting this chart up in the lounge or team area.

4. Show parents how to use this method and put a chart up in the volunteer center or other spot where parents gather. This can be used for things like summer activity suggestions, home discipline, or homework issues, and so forth. The whole community, staff and parents alike, can offer suggestions.

Selected References

Osborn (1963), Gibbs (2001), Annenberg Institute for School Reform (1998), Texas Department of Education (2006), Chang and Dalziel (1999a), Bennett and Rolheiser (2001).

GRAFFITI BOARD: AN EXAMPLE

Create a small group of trained "New Friends"

Develop a notebook with "everything you need to know about being in this class"

Suggest a schoolwide orientation program for new students. It would save time on tours and the "how to find" phase.

Use a getting-to-know-you activity; it never hurts to build team even after the start of the school year.

Problem: 5 new students entered my class within the last two days. What are some ways to rapidly get them used to the rules and routines without disrupting the class?

Ask PTA to create welcome baskets with school calendars, agendas, newspaper, how to get needs met and some school supplies and treats. Realtors often do this for new families to the area.

Notify real estate office or Chamber and see if they can get us welcome baskets for the whole family.

STRATEGY 40

Hot Buttons

Purpose: Building Resilience and Creating Solutions

This process addresses the need for an active method of managing conflict and building resilience in successful teams. Once teams are established, they go through certain stages as they encounter stressful circumstances. This method seeks to address those stopping points in a humorous way.

Basics

Number of Participants	Small groups of 2 to 12
Time Needed	20 minutes to two hours depending on the number in the group; larger groups take longer
Room Arrangement	Tables and chairs
Difficulty Level	Moderate level, to be used with an existing team that has already formed a working level of trust
Brain Bits	People need social relationships that validate and result in acceptance; we need to use "sense-making" actions to move forward in our learning; people need trustworthy environments in which to work and grow
Adult Learning Principle	Adults need to connect to what they do well, see the real-life use in learning, and have their unique circumstances acknowledged
Materials	Template for sharing or chart paper and markers
Other	A lower risk version without the "hot" part of the getting to know you works well with creating a growth-oriented climate for teams. Such strategies as "Find Someone Who," "A-B-C Conversations," and "Random Partners" work well

Process Directions

1. Orient the group to the purpose.

2. Each participant creates a poster on chart paper or other large paper.

3. On that paper:
   a. The participant notes things that he or she feels are absolutely critical to the success of the team.
   b. Then list things that make the team get off track, stuck, or stressed in some way.
   c. List things that make him or her personally feel accomplishment as part of the team.

    d. List things that are "Hot Buttons" that make him or her uncomfortable, that make him or her feel like time is wasted, or that make the participant angry when the team does these things.

    e. Draw a symbol for a well-functioning team.

4. Each participant presents his or her poster.

5. Discuss common needs and success indicators. The awareness of each participant's point of view about successful and unsuccessful team behaviors works well to push most teams forward beyond a difficult phase.

When

- Use for getting a group unstuck.
- Use if going in a new direction.
- Use when dealing with conflict.
- Use to deal with stress in time, resources, or people.
- Use to help with high or increasing "must-do" workload.

Examples and Uses

1. A team is struggling to complete tasks against a deadline.

2. A team gets off task frequently or does not accomplish stated work.

3. There may be some minor conflict or stress between members.

4. A team finishes a project and is about to start a new one.

Selected References

Beaudoin and Taylor (2004), Daniels (1986), Destra Consulting Group (2002), National School Board Association (2005), Roberts and Pruitt (2003).

HOT BUTTONS

These things/actions are critical to the success of our team:	These things/actions pull our team off task:
When our team . . . I feel a real sense of accomplishment!	These are my "Hot Buttons" on our team!
This is my symbol for a well-functioning team:	

STRATEGY 41

Journey Mapping
(Also Known as Histo-Mapping)

Purpose: Building Resilience and Creating Solutions

Retracing the steps of the past is a great way to gain insight into important information that could otherwise be lost. It is a visual, pictorial way to record history. It highlights events, key strategies, and pitfalls that we need to be aware of as we plan next steps.

Basics

Number of Participants	Whole faculty or small groups
Time Needed	40–60 minutes
Room Arrangement	Small groups or one larger one around a wall chart
Difficulty Level	Easier with prior preparation; see suggestions in directions
Brain Bits	Increase social and emotional richness of a group and sustain the resilience of staff even through times of change
Adult Learning Principle	Honors the history and experiences of existing staff, orients new staff, makes connections between the old and new
Materials	Chart paper, markers, and optional artifacts
Other	Could be used with "Current Snapshot"
	With a newly formed group use "Journey Mapping" in the Creating a Growth-Oriented Climate section; this method of journey mapping works better with established groups or new groups where trust is less of a concern. This method also addresses the "plate is full" issue that comes from piling on initiatives over time by helping groups decide what to keep

Process Directions

1. Explain the purpose; it is helpful to look to the past prior to looking toward the future. Put out a notice about two weeks ahead or in an opening letter to staff. Ask veteran staff to bring any artifacts to help tell the story on the particular topic to be discussed. Jotting down some notes on what we remember, student work samples, plans, pictures, influential quotes, old agendas, and so forth all are helpful.

2. Break the large group into small groups, each tackling an area on the Journey Map into the past.

3. Use "Gallery Walk" or "Round the Room Brainstorming" to add ideas, facts, or artifacts to the initial work of each group.

4. Put up a chart for each area depicting the history. Discuss the completed work and how it will help us plan.

5. Create a future plan by putting up the same charts with the same headings.

When

- This method honors using the past to create the future or avoid pitfalls in the future.
- You need to orient new staff to the work and values of a school or team.
- The group needs a humorous and fun way to celebrate our progress to date.
- Use prior to future planning of major initiatives and complex projects for which there is substantial history, anticipated resistance, or questions as to why the new work must be done.

Examples and Uses

1. Standards-based education: what have we done so far. This is good to do before launching into Power Standard identification or other refinements of the standards-based curriculum you now use.

2. About to launch into performance assessment design? It is best to know what rubrics already exist, what training existing staff had, and the wisdom level in the building. Do students know how to use rubrics and models? What impact has this had, and what is the desired impact?

3. History of grading in a building is a powerful way to renew efforts in interrater reliability. What is the current and perhaps diverse distinction between A's and B's and so on? What happens if a student doesn't demonstrate a grade-level indicator the first time it is assessed, and how is that graded?

Selected References

Bailey (1995), Chadwick (2006), Chang and Dalziel (1999b), Gregory and Kuzmich (2004), Roberts and Pruitt (2003), Wald and Castleberry (2000).

JOURNEY MAPPING

Sample Components of a Journey Map

1. Timeline of Events or Initiatives

Example: Reading Materials

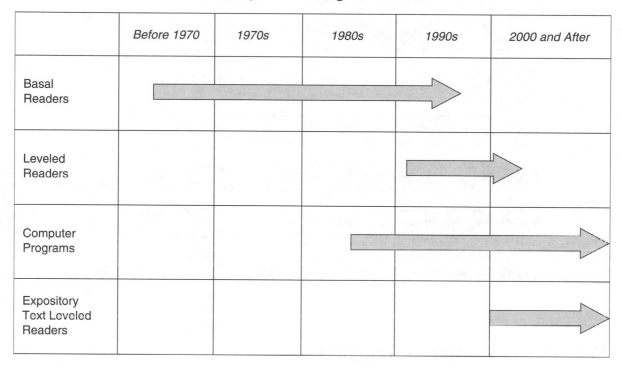

	Before 1970	*1970s*	*1980s*	*1990s*	*2000 and After*
Basal Readers					
Leveled Readers					
Computer Programs					
Expository Text Leveled Readers					

2. The Shape of Professional Development

Examples!

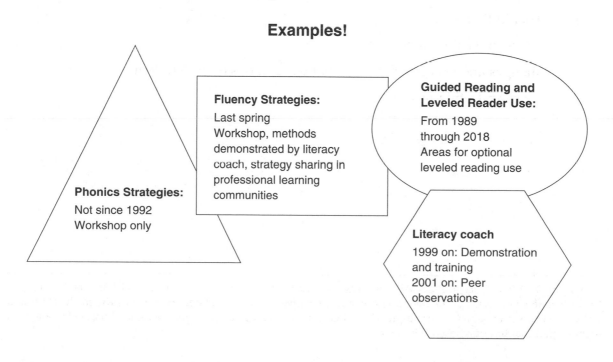

Phonics Strategies:
Not since 1992
Workshop only

Fluency Strategies:
Last spring
Workshop, methods demonstrated by literacy coach, strategy sharing in professional learning communities

Guided Reading and Leveled Reader Use:
From 1989 through 2018
Areas for optional leveled reading use

Literacy coach
1999 on: Demonstration and training
2001 on: Peer observations

3. Student Assessment Results

Example of State Assessment Results in Reading

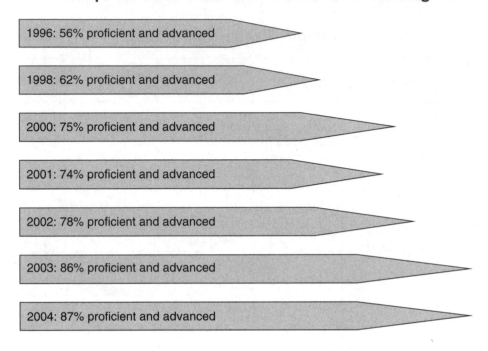

1996: 56% proficient and advanced

1998: 62% proficient and advanced

2000: 75% proficient and advanced

2001: 74% proficient and advanced

2002: 78% proficient and advanced

2003: 86% proficient and advanced

2004: 87% proficient and advanced

Our Areas for Journey Mapping

1. Resource allocation

2. Leadership distribution

3. District initiatives

4. Changes in legal requirements

5. Challenges and successes with special populations of our students

6. Other contributing factors

JOURNEY MAPPING OUR FUTURE

Given Our Map of the Past . . .

1. Timeline

Plot out the journey you wish to take over the next two to three years given what you have accomplished.

Example: Add components in technological reading and writing; increase inferential comprehension by introducing student strategies versus materials.

2. Professional Development

Given the current steps, what would be logical next steps?

Examples: Ongoing assistance for new teachers; add lesson studies or student portfolios.

3. Assessment Results

Where would you like student results to be in two to three years?

Examples: 90% to 95% of our students will achieve at the proficient or advanced level, increased performance of special education students, and so forth.

Add Other Journey Mapping Components as Needed

1. Resources we need

2. Time we need

3. People we need

4. Communication with parents

5. District support

6. Outside resources

7. Ways to address our challenges

8. Other components for our success

STRATEGY 42

Musical Chairs

Purpose: Building Resilience and Creating Solutions

This method is a great way to share ideas and honor the wisdom of the group. Whenever adults can share the great things they are doing, help a colleague, and get assistance solving a problem, they build resilience and high-performing teams. This is also referred to as "consulting line" when used to share great ideas and strategies.

Basics

Number of Participants	12 to 150 people
Time Needed	15–40 minutes (depends on number of rounds)
Room Arrangement	Floor space for lines of people
Difficulty Level	Easy
Brain Bits	Making personal connections, using what we know, establishing patterns, and using conscious language for team understanding are all supportive of adult learning and sustain that learning
Adult Learning Principle	Adults like hands-on and interactive activities to engage in with real-life applications
Materials	Chairs, something to play music, a music CD
Other	With really large groups, you can form two groups of two rows

Process Directions

1. Say, "Given a particular topic (such as differentiation, literacy across content areas, or strategies to increase math problem solving), we are going to share the expertise in this room."

2. Form two lines or rows with half the participants in each line, and then face each other in line. Label one Row A and one Row B. Have them bring chairs.

3. Row A asks a question about the given topic. The questions can be about something that is a challenge or dilemma, something they want to know more about, or a problem they want help solving.

4. Row B gives advice, offers suggestions, and shares what works.

5. Then reverse roles: The person in Row B asks questions, and the Row A person acts as a personal coach, offering ideas, encouragement, and suggestions.

6. Give each question-and-answer interaction about three to four minutes, so each round takes about six to eight minutes.

7. Then move the first person from one end of Row B to the other end of the Row B and have everyone shift over one person in Row B. Play music to signal the rotation.

8. Repeat the process in Numbers 3 through 6.

9. Rotate as time allows. Use music to signal each rotation.

10. Process the process as well as the great ideas. Sample process questions:
    a. How might this work with students?
    b. What if we used this process once a quarter at the end or start of a staff meeting?
    c. What are one or two great ideas you got from your peers?
    d. What other ways could we use the expertise in our group, team, or school?

When

- Use to sustain the resilience of the group.
- Use when sharing expertise between multiple learning communities.
- Use to share your learning from your own professional growth.

Examples and Uses

1. Use with a PLC in which each member has done practice with strategies for literacy.

2. Use for sharing strategies for cooperative groups.

3. Use when problem solving around highly mobile students.

4. Use when comparing strategies for reducing re-teaching and increasing long-term memory.

5. This can be used for interviewing your partner about what he or she is doing with assessments, English-Language learners, or discipline issues in the classroom.

6. This is also good for sharing knowledge and best practices.

Selected References

Annenberg Institute for School Reform (1998), Australian Government Department of Education (2006), Chadwick (2006), Gibbs (2001).

MUSICAL CHAIRS

Arrange participants in two rows facing one another close enough for conversation.

Directions

1. Ask participants in Row A to select a topic, issue, or problem to share with their partner in Row B.

2. Partners in Row B have two to four minutes to provide suggestions to Row A partner. The person in Row A can record ideas.

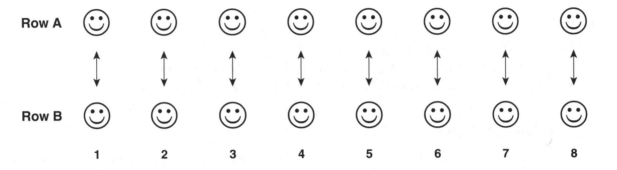

3. Reverse roles. The person in Row B shares a problem and records suggestions. The person in Row A gives suggestions (2–4 minutes).

4. Rotate participants. Ask the first person in Row B to move to the last chair in the row. All other Row B participants move one seat to the right. Play music while this is occurring, and turn it off during the coaching time.

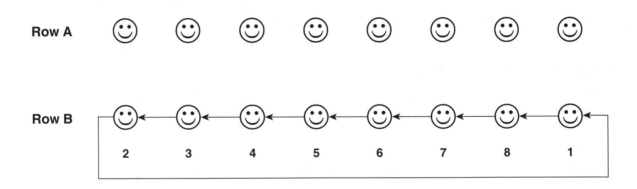

5. Repeat Steps 2 to 4 so each rotation is with a new partner.

6. Participants review suggestions and select ideas to implement.

STRATEGY 43

Parking Lot

Purpose: Building Resilience and Creating Solutions

Problem solving on a regular basis is important work for learning communities. Getting individual needs met is also important to the overall resilience of the group.

Basics

Number of Participants	Any number
Time Needed	5–15 minutes at end of a session or meeting
Room Arrangement	Any
Difficulty Level	Easy for participants
Brain Bits	Adults have a curiosity about topics they seek out and want to get their needs met; questions that get answered on any given learning topic are likely to be more transferable for the participant; solving problems is essential for actual use of learning
Adult Learning Principle	Life applicability is a critical learning principle as well as connecting new learning to what we already know or are curious about
Materials	Sticky notes, chart paper
Other	For larger trainings or longer team meetings, you could process answers to questions at one-hour intervals rather than at the end of the session

Process Directions

1. Put up a chart paper and title it "Parking Lot."

2. Make certain to have sticky notes for participants.

3. If at any time during the meeting or when learning participants have questions or issues that were not addressed, they write them on the sticky note and place it on the Parking Lot chart. A burning issue or concern is also appropriate to write down.

4. Take time at the end of the meeting. Read the notes and invite the rest of the group to help answer the question or address an issue. Get two to three responses for each note and move to the next one.

5. Optional step: More complex issues might be placed on the agenda for the next meeting or learning session. Participants could help find information or solutions prior to the next session.

When

- Use for solving problems.
- Use when addressing "hot issues" before they interfere with the progress of the team.
- Use to sharing strategies and solutions.
- Use when answering questions that were not yet addressed.

Examples and Uses

1. The PLC is doing a book study and agrees to try to implement two strategies before the next meeting. A question about how to get it done given an upcoming assembly or assessment period might need to be answered. Or getting advice from peers on selecting which two strategies to use for a particular subgroup might be the most helpful.

2. A shared decision-making team is meeting on budget allocation issues. A Parking Lot issue might include advice on how to get buy-in from staff who are not present or from parents on the advisory committee.

3. The topic is on writing across content areas. A Parking Lot issue might be on how to grade or give credit in content-area classes other than English.

Selected References

Deal and Peterson (1998), Garmston (1997), Roberts and Pruitt (2003), Wald and Castleberry (2000).

PARKING LOT:

Suggestions and Examples

PLACE QUESTIONS HERE

PLACE "HOT" ISSUES HERE

PLACE SUGGESTIONS HERE

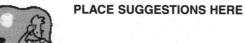

STRATEGY 44

Roadblock Removal

Purpose: Building Resilience and Creating Solutions

This is a proactive strategy that builds on the successful removal of roadblocks at the start of a new initiative, project, or phase of learning. Reflecting on how we removed roadblocks to success in previous projects and then consciously seeking to prevent such roadblocks on the next project is a good way to replicate success.

Basics

Number of Participants	Small groups of three to eight
Time Needed	15–20 minutes
Room Arrangement	Table and chairs
Difficulty Level	Easy and low risk
Brain Bits	Adults need to feel successful and easily seek repeating that success; building on the known to support the unknown is also a natural desire of adult thinking
Adult Learning Principle	Making connections with what we know and using our direct experiences as a rich source of information helps us to move forward
Materials	Template or chart paper and markers
Other	This works well for low-controversy work that is coming up and teams with a good level of resilience; if there is resistance, use "Force Field" instead of this activity

Process Directions

1. List a success you had recently.
2. Now brainstorm a list of roadblocks you have encountered or things that hindered your forward progress.
3. Since you were successful with this goal or project, you must have removed the roadblocks. How did you do that?
4. Given what you learned from your success, what roadblocks or hindrances do you anticipate on this next project or goal?

5. Using what you learned during your recent success, how could you prevent these roadblocks or more easily deal with them?

6. Finally, how will you monitor the roadblocks and forward momentum of your next project or goal?

When

- Use just before starting a new project, goal, or phase of a project.
- Use when a difficult but successful goal is completed.
- Use when unanticipated roadblocks arise or the rate of change is high around the topic or issue you are trying to impact.

Examples and Uses

1. You have successfully created assessments for narrative writing and are going to tackle expository writing next.

2. You are adopting new course or content materials. What did you learn from the previous adoption?

3. Your assessment results for special-education students in reading are finally improving, and you are about to tackle another subgroup.

4. A group of teachers shared strategies for differentiation that were quite effective. Results of student assessment on unit tests and other less-formal measures improved. This PLC wants to continue to add strategies to its toolkit.

Selected References

Gregory and Kuzmich (2005a, 2005b).

ROADBLOCK REMOVAL

> **What was our recent success?**

> **What roadblocks did we encounter?**
>
>
>
>
>
>
> **How did we deal with the roadblocks and get rid of them (or not let them stop us)?**

> **What is our upcoming work?**
>
>
>
> **How could we prevent roadblocks or more easily remove them in our upcoming work?**
>
>
>
> **How will we monitor our success and momentum?**

Source: Gregory and Kuzmich (2005b).

Removing Roadblocks: An Example

What was our recent success?

We improved our questioning strategies for students and teachers, and this focus on thinking skills helped us increase our reading comprehension scores and our math numeracy scores.

What roadblocks did we encounter?

Teacher questioning changed, but not student questioning.
  Teachers were not certain how to increase or improve student questioning.

How did we deal with roadblocks and get rid of them (or not let them stop us)?

We did a study of parts of two books and viewed some videotape examples of strategies to expand our teaching toolkit around questioning. We changed our strategies to get students to formulate more questions and gave them question starters. We also helped students deepen their thinking and question their assumptions across content areas.

What Is our upcoming work?

We want to increase student use of editing strategies for all types of writing. We want to improve our assessment results in writing for all students.

How could we prevent roadblocks or easily remove them in our upcoming work?

We need to plan for the professional development at the start of this year to increase our teacher toolkit with strategies that help the teacher and show the student how to take responsibility for editing.
  We may also encounter grading issues, and we need to talk about that as soon as we run into problems. Solutions may include developing quick-grading techniques that again focus the responsibility for editing on students.

How will we monitor our success and momentum?

We are going to meet twice a month; at least once a month, we need ask ourselves what the issues and roadblocks are and seek solutions immediately.

The Question Matters

Reviewing Student Work

Purpose: Building Resilience and Creating Solutions

Reviewing student work is critical to getting results. There are numerous approaches to that work. The strategies in this section help learning communities and critical friends groups approach the work with good questions. What we ask for is what we get. It is essential that we learn to ask the right questions about student work.

Basics

Number of Participants	Small groups
Time Needed	1–2 hours
Room Arrangement	Table and chairs with access to chart paper or white board
Difficulty Level	Difficult
Brain Bits	People need social relationships that validate and result in acceptance; we need to use "sense-making" actions to move forward in our learning; people need trustworthy environments in which to work and grow
Adult Learning Principle	Adults need to connect to what they do well, see the real-life use in learning, and have their unique circumstances acknowledged
Materials	Chart paper and markers, student work, rubrics, anchor papers or work
Other	Create a bank of question stems for the group to use over time; this set of questions can be content or grade-level specific and reflect various levels of analysis and planning

Process Directions

1. Start reviewing student work by sharing the prompt or assessment that was used with students, the rubric, and any models used to teach students. (It is suggested that

student work samples be selected, such as two samples of nonproficient work, two of proficient work, and two of advanced work. Or, two or three exemplars from each scoring level on the rubric could be selected. Limiting the number of projects or work samples is a more effective use of group time in initial planning. The teacher may need to apply the process to all examples; however, the group may not have the time to use more than eight examples effectively in a 90-minute to two-hour block of time.)

2. Share results with the team. Decide what worked and what did not.

3. Form a question that you would like answered to address what did not work as well as anticipated.

4. Work through a protocol (a few are listed in the following) to find the answer about student work.

5. List next steps to take in the classroom as a result of the attempt to answer the critical question and plan actions together.

6. Review results at the next meeting.

When

- A well-established team is ready to use higher risk data sources such as student work.
- A group wants to close achievement gaps as rapidly as possible.
- A group has already created scoring guides and knows how to use models and anchor papers or projects with students.
- A group has enough time together to conduct an effective review.

Examples and Uses

1. Goal is to improve expository writing among subgroup populations.

2. We need to get more effective science experiment analyses from students.

3. This could be used to improve the quality and depth of thinking for social studies debates.

4. We want to get students to set better goals for fitness and follow through on those goals as they log progress.

5. Demonstration of the application of multiple strategies to solve math problems is needed.

Selected References

Annenberg Institute for School Reform (1998); Langer, Colton, and Goff (2003); NCREL (2006); National School Reform Faculty Harmony Center (2005).

DEVELOPING GOOD CRITICAL QUESTIONS FOR REVIEWING STUDENT WORK

Use these question formulation cards to help you. Using one or two of these to guide your review of student work may help you get the results you seek.

Formulate a question about the rubric:

Formulate a question about the anchor or model papers/projects:

Formulate a question about whether the scoring was correct (Is outstanding really outstanding?):

Formulate a question about the strategies for teaching or learning that resulted in these student-work examples:

Formulate a question about what it would take for students to move to the next level of performance:

Formulate a question about whether these samples of student work demonstrate sufficient growth over time:

Examples of Critical Questions to Ask About Student Work Samples

1. Does this work sample or performance tell us how well the student has demonstrated a standard or benchmark?

2. Did our rubric give the student enough information to be successful?

3. Was the student able to utilize the exemplars to correct his or her work to a level of proficient or better?

4. Do we have agreement among ourselves about what quality work looks like?

5. What practices or strategies caused certain students to be successful?

6. What research could we do, training could we take, or coaching could we get that would help more students demonstrate proficiency on the standards?

Looking at Student Work

Additional questions that help us think diagnostically and plan for future learning and growth:

- Which subgroups (learning disabled, gifted, and minority) did better; which did not? What adjustments were developed for each group? How well did these strategies work?

- What was the level of critical thinking students demonstrated? Did it match the standards? Did it match the prompt and the rubric or scoring guide? Did you preassess for this? Did students receive instruction and learning opportunities at this level of thinking prior to the final assessment?

- What did the section or items of the assignment or assessment look like in terms of student performance? Do you have other evidence confirming that this is an accurate picture of students' level of performance?

- What might have caused these results? Look at time spent learning, resources utilized, strategies for both learning and instruction, and whether staff had adequate training, coaching, and preparation to accomplish the goals of the unit or lesson.

CRITICAL FACTORS FOR REVIEWING STUDENT WORK

Collaborative: Do it with colleagues; the work is hard and meant to be done with others in a job-embedded manner. Use protocols from National Staff Development Council, Critical Friends Groups, and numerous other resources.

Utilize Collaborative Scoring: Share a common rubric or scoring method, develop it, and refine it together. Make certain the challenge level and thinking levels are correct. Don't put direction items in rubric form. Build rubrics around key concepts or critical questions.

Develop Exemplars: Update and share exemplars. Each year, double-check that the exemplars and anchor papers or projects reflect the right levels of performance. Set expectations too low by selecting the wrong exemplars and students will not demonstrate sufficient growth.

Share Your Conclusions and Results: Replicate success by sharing what works with new teachers and with other school and district teams.

Focused Strategy Discussions: Focus on increasing the number of students who reach or exceed the standard. Share and coach peers on best practices that get results.

STRATEGY 46

Two Sides of the Story

Purpose: Building Resilience and Creating Solutions

"Two Sides of the Story" is a great method for getting controversial subjects out in the open. Looking at multiple viewpoints ahead of planning or implementation better ensures the success of a project or work plan.

Basics

Number of Participants	Smaller groups of 6 to 12 or larger group of 12 to 50
Time Needed	40–50 minutes
Room Arrangement	Small groups will need tables and chairs
Difficulty Level	Moderate, takes careful understanding of the directions
Brain Bits	Helps connect and prioritize
Adult Learning Principle	Supports adult need for choice and real-life application
Materials	Chart paper and markers
Other	You can do this with a whole staff and split the group in two or take a professional learning community and split it in two smaller groups

Process Directions

1. State the issue at hand.

2. Review the directions with the group.
   a. Split the larger or smaller group into two parts.
   b. Each part goes to the corner of a large room or two different rooms and brainstorms a list of reasons *for* an issue.
   c. Allow about eight minutes for this.
   d. Then each group lists reasons *against* an issue.
   e. Again, take about eight minutes to complete this brainstorm list.

3. Each of the two groups reports on their reasons for and against the issue.

4. The facilitator has each group look at their second list (against).
   a. The group examines the items that were negative or deterrents to solving the issue or implementing a solution.
   b. The group decides who will do what in the investigation.
   c. Then the group members go find out information and facts to see if these items can be overcome.

5. Present those findings at the next meeting.
   a. Decide at the second meeting if the deterrents to the solution have been addressed and whether it is worth it to proceed.
   b. For topics of high controversy, use "Force Field" or "Nominal Group Process" to help with the decision-making process.

When

- Buy-in is essential to the success of a controversial initiative or project.
- Resistance is already evident.
- There are competing large projects and the staff needs a decision-making process to choose which project has the greatest payoff or potential for success.

Examples and Uses

1. Staff are trying to decide whether to start on differentiation strategies to meet diverse student needs or initiate a new discipline program.

2. Reading and writing across content areas has been proposed as an area of focus. Some of the content-area teachers are uncertain as to how to fit this into an already crowded schedule.

3. Implementation of materials or strategies is required, and staff have a choice of methods for getting this started. This might be the case with the adoption of new textbooks or materials approved by the Board of Education.

Selected References

Burke (1993), Chadwick (2006), Chang and Buster (1999), Costa and Garmston (2002), Daniels (1986), Deal and Peterson (2002), Johnson et al. (1991a, 1991b), Roberts and Pruitt (2003).

TWO SIDES OF THE STORY

Topic:

Reasons <u>For</u>   **Reasons <u>Against</u>**

Determining Priorities and Creating Excellence

Dramatic movement [happens when] myriad initiatives have started to unfold. They represent powerful, yet still incremental movement within the operational framework. The pace of these changes may be breathtaking . . . initiatives come in surges of overlapping efforts. These kinds of changes have a major impact on how an organization functions.

—Daryl Conner (1998, p. 78)

TRANSITIONING WITH MULTIPLE INITIATIVES

This section of the book is about the strategies that help us through the long-term process we call "responsive change." Responsive change means that we look at the results of our actions and seek to creatively impact the level of excellence in those results. We know that change is continual in this century. We certainly experienced a glimpse of this over the last 15 years. So instead of sustaining one eventful change at a time, numerous changes come our way simultaneously. It also seems that we go through these cycles more and more frequently.

The old linear models of managing change do not work in this era. Older methods assume we are dealing with one thing at a time, perhaps one data point, and that we have infinite time to get "good" at the latest change. The reality of great schools is that they have learned how to help people through the process rather than the event.

Great schools learn how to view change as a continual crafting process coupled with periods of high creativity and problem solving. They actively create the vision of excellence in their school as an ongoing, living process rather than a mission statement set in one time-frame. This is rewarding work, and we want to give you the strategies to sustain your ongoing journey toward excellence for our students.

Aristotle said, "We are what we repeatedly do. Excellence, then, is not an act but a habit."

Teams get started on something new, and there is a transition or transformation that occurs. We have to figure out what to give up, what to focus on, how to manage the limitations of our time and other resources, and how to create and evaluate solutions. William Bridges and Susan Mitchell (2000) discuss the need to help people continually "reorient" to the changes. They caution us that for a new initiative to work, the process of creating the change will take a while, longer than it took to decide to change. Teams need the time and support to experiment creatively with the possibilities and the results. Peter Senge et al. (1999) write about piloting new ideas, and Daryl Conner (1998) writes about building organizational "nimbleness" through allowing trials and discussions.

RESPONSIVE CHANGE

Teams cycle through periods of predictability, and then, as they decide on a new course, move into a period of instability or cognitive dissonance. In the last section of the book, we have discussed how to overcome resistance that sometimes occurs at the start of this phase. However, once this initial resistance passes, how we focus the creative energy of the team is critical. We have discovered that four major types of strategies help groups provide the support needed to transition toward what Conner (1993) called "Dramatic Movement" and we call responsive change.

- Setting priorities: Prioritization of the work helps provide some comforting structure and much-needed focus as people move in and out of this transition phase.
- Storytelling: Generating the fluidity and flexibility in thinking needed for creative solutions, on multiple fronts, requires an atmosphere of both experimentation and of storytelling.
- Adapting to results: We need to act upon results from the initial trials of a new implementation and adjust our practices toward the excellence we desire for students and ourselves.

- Goal setting: Learning about fluid goal setting for the team and for individuals that is adjusted with both organizational and personal realities in mind helps us see results sooner.

We have included team strategies that help move the dialogue and shift actions as the "initiative surges" occur. This allows a team to become more adaptive to change and to view excellence as a process, not a destination. These strategies help groups with overlapping projects and issues to limit "initiative fatigue" that Doug Reeves (2002) cautions us about.

SETTING PRIORITIES

The military realized in ancient and modern times that a critical path exists for getting complex work done on time and with deep concern for the personal well-being of its greatest asset, people. In times of overlapping changes, we need to help teams decide what is critical and what is just "background noise." This helps retain the energy of a learning community and not waste valuable time and personal capability on too many targets at once. Reeves concludes that "the law of initiative fatigue states that as fixed resources (time, resources, physical and emotional energy of staff) are divided into a growing number of initiatives, the time allowed for each initiative declines at a constant rate" (2002, p. 83). Therefore, if we can teach groups to find that critical path and those high-priority areas, we can focus the work and adaptability of the team as we move forward on multiple initiatives. Strategies such as the "People Ladder" and the "Impact of Solutions" help us create that achievable path to excellence.

STORYTELLING

In the previous sections, we discuss the importance of history, ritual, and celebration in helping teams form, norm, and storm. To effectively move toward the performances we need for success, storytelling is a great way to help us cope with the uncertainty of experimentation and the newness of implementing changes. Storytelling helps us connect the past and future. It helps us lower the risk as we move through trial and error of implementation. Storytelling can help us describe what did not work and help us remember to celebrate even the smallest improvements. In addition, we know that we must work on multiple issues, and storytelling helps us integrate those initiatives so that we focus on the journey of the child, not just the "to-do" list of the staff. Turning lesson studies and unit studies into a story helps us see the interconnection of actions and results. Telling the stories needed to complete a "Probable and Preferred Future" helps us reduce the anxiety about next steps.

ADAPTING TO RESULTS

If we forget to celebrate and to build upon what worked, we are doomed to longer and longer planning phases with shorter and shorter implementation phases. We need more time in implementing a change than deciding to change. It is more critical and creates faster results to learn from successes than to analyze to death the failures. It is a mistake we make too frequently as we get groups to review data. If we just ask groups what they see in the data, they tend to focus on the negative. We propose that results occur more rapidly when you look at what worked, celebrate that, and decide how to use what you learned from that success to create the next success. So we offer strategies such as the "DIP Party," "Building on Success," "Celebrations and Next Steps," and "Cause-and-Effect Planning." It has always been known that we should accent the positive. Focusing on the "doughnut and not the hole" is a catchy saying that makes good sense. Both of these notions reinforce the need to receive positive feedback in safe environments to raise endorphins in the brain and to have high expectations through lofty goals.

GOAL SETTING

Teams that set goals for incremental success do more to chip away at excellence for students than learning teams that set lofty long-range goals. Such incremental progress is desirable given the structure of accountability in today's schools. School teams encounter so many overlapping initiatives that it is critical to create points of time that we can say something is finished or in place. Such goal setting might be that our priorities are chosen and we can celebrate that step. Goals about sharing what works and collecting a number of strategies for our teaching toolkit might be another opportunity to commemorate. Getting two more students to be proficient on a unit assessment *is* a cause for celebration. It is very important that we don't just set goals for learning communities around annual targets, but that we celebrate the journey to excellence along the way. If excellence is an ongoing process and not a single event, then we should have small continual targets that we can reach and celebrate. That helps teams sustain the effort and renew their energy over the long haul of continual change. So, we offer you strategies such as KWL and "the Interview" as well as others to help you create those celebration opportunities.

THE FUTURE FOCUS

In large part, we belong to a global learning community that changes moment by moment on a scale we can hardly make rational sense of today. The skills we need to work together on behalf of our students and our future are changing. Sustaining the energy and momentum of a team makes us proud to be a part of the journey. Jennifer James tells us, "As increasing self-knowledge expands our individuality, the shrinking globe and marketplace will pull us together and increase our interdependence. . . . The skills to think in the future tense will be imperative" (1996, p. 229). The journey for our learning communities is not about what was, but what can be for each student entrusted to us. We hope our strategies help you reach out to the future you can create through responsive change.

PRIMARY PURPOSE FOR THE STRATEGIES IN THIS SECTION

In this chapter, we offer you strategies to determine priorities and create excellence over time including:

- Goal setting
- Tying data to practice
- Analyzing results
- Limiting "initiative fatigue"
- Determining excellence

STRATEGY 47

Building on Success

Purpose: Determining Priorities and Creating Excellence

When faced with an array of needs, knowing how to create a target for excellence is essential for successful results. This method helps build those priorities by reviewing recent successes and reflecting on how those successes were accomplished. Then staff applies that same set of strategies to the new initiative. Learning to replicate success is a key factor for model and highly successful schools and teams.

Basics

Number of Participants	Small groups of 2 to 8 or a larger group of up to 20
Time Needed	45–60 minutes
Room Arrangement	Small groups in chairs around chart stands
Difficulty Level	With clear directions and an example or two, this process is of moderate difficulty
Brain Bits	Emotionally, adults need challenging tasks with a minimum of threat or risk to learn or create Reflective practice and dialogue helps us sustain learning and initiatives
Adult Learning Principle	Experientially, adults need to connect new ideas or actions to what we know and do well. Performance-centered adults need opportunities for reflection.
Materials	Chart paper and markers
Other	Works well to have at least some members of the team or group who know the history of what has been successful in this school or for this team

Process Directions

1. Brainstorm a list of very specific successes that the team or school has created. Record these on chart paper large enough for all to see.

2. Divide the large group into small teams; give each group chart paper and markers. Assign each group one of the successes.

3. Small groups brainstorm the actions that were taken to cause the success. What was done? How were resources allocated? What made this success possible?

4. Each small group reports out. Before that happens, ask participants to listen for common themes and actions.

5. As a whole group, list the common themes and actions on a chart.

6. Now apply these strategies and actions to a new initiative or action that needs to be taken. After creating the new goal, these common actions and themes should help a group form the backbone of an action plan.

When

- Use before completing a new action plan for the school year.
- Use when tackling a new critical question for a team.
- Use after successful completion of one step in a larger process and ready to plan and complete the next step.
- Use when building resilience of staff by focusing on what we do well and how to replicate that success.

Examples and Uses

1. Last year, the school was successful in bringing up expository reading comprehension across subgroups. Highlighting what was done for that success, the group uses those steps to improve vocabulary or the next aspect of reading.

2. During the first quarter of the year, discipline for physical aggression is reduced. Utilize some of the same successful practices to now address bullying behaviors.

3. Staff feel overwhelmed as state assessments loom in the early spring. Celebrate the successes of the first half of the year. Now talk about how those actions will positively impact the results on the assessments and how to apply those actions to the challenges of the second half of the year.

Selected References

Gregory and Kuzmich (2005a, 2005b).

BUILDING ON SUCCESS

Questions to Guide Our Inventory of Successful Practices

Name your success as specifically as possible.

What was done?

How were resources allocated?

What factors made this success possible?

Are there any other reasons for success?

BUILDING ON SUCCESS: AN EXAMPLE

Questions to Guide Our Inventory of Successful Practices

Name your success as specifically as possible.

Reading scores went up for Hispanic learners at our high school for two years in a row, at a higher rate than other groups. The gap between Hispanic learners and others is closing rapidly.

What was done?

- Every teacher helped plan what reading and writing would look like across content areas.
- We did several book studies around adolescent literacy.
- We sent teacher leaders to workshops and training on literacy; they came back and taught everyone.
- Students learned multiple strategies to help them access text of any kind.

How were resources allocated?

- Professional development money, including books for all teachers and ongoing professional development
- Job-embedded professional development, including release of three teacher leaders in literacy for one to two periods per day to coach the rest of the staff.
- Time was scheduled each week to work in professional learning communities by department or grade level to share and develop expertise around strategies and student work.
- Development of common scoring for expository text comprehension and writing, complete with content-specific models

What factors made this success possible?

- Embedded and ongoing staff development
- Time and money targeted
- Students learning strategies to help themselves
- Peer coaching
- Development of a common, schoolwide vocabulary and set of strategies

Are there any other reasons for success?

- Supportive leadership of teachers, school administrators, and district staff
- Ongoing dialogue about best practices and student growth throughout the school year
- Celebration of small, successful steps along the way

Cause-and-Effect Planning

Purpose: Determining Priorities and Creating Excellence

This processing method helps staff focus on the underlying causes for the current data results and then helps them plan to change or redirect those causes. If your reading scores are low, it is important to know what the causes are to best select next steps that will build the foundation for better results.

Basics

Number of Participants	Small groups of up to eight
Time Needed	45–60 minutes
Room Arrangement	Tables for small groups, chairs
Difficulty Level	Easy with a few examples
Brain Bits	Emotional impact and social support and positive feedback, conscious format to focus attention and increase memory, reflective practice
Adult Learning Principle	Meets needs to build off what we know and then connect to new learning, opportunities for reflection with peers
Materials	Two sheets of chart paper and some markers for each group, tape
Other	Two-part process, takes about 20 minutes for each part and about 10 minutes for processing Model each part first or hand out examples

Process Directions

1. Choose a specific area of focus from a body of evidence, such as algebraic concepts in math, word choice in writing, or success of strategies to address student tardiness.

2. Divide a sheet of chart paper into six sections with room for a heading. Label the sections: time, resources, strategies, expectations, professional development, and other.

3. Have groups work for about 15 to 20 minutes listing one to three causes for the underlying specific result.

4. Create a second chart paper with the same labels as in Number 2.

5. Have groups work for about 20 minutes to list possible actions to take that would address the causes listed on the previous chart.

6. Report out on possible changes in each of the six areas. You now have the beginning of a plan for the next year.

7. Keep both charts and use them to discuss progress throughout the year.

When

- Use after looking at the data at the beginning of the school year.
- Use at the end of the school year, using the data from that year.
- Students' results are not where you would like them.

Examples and Uses

1. Math or literacy scores did not go up as anticipated.
2. Discipline referrals went up for drug use or absences increased.
3. Parent satisfaction rate decreased.
4. Learning teams did not reach specific goals as planned.
5. Students cannot correct writing using a model and or use a scoring guide to produce proficient work.

Selected Reference

Gregory and Kuzmich (2004).

CHART 1

Cause-and-Effect Analysis

Area of Concern: _____

Time	Resources: materials, people, equipment, etc.
Strategies: teaching, learning, assessment	**Professional Development**
Expectations of Staff	**Other Factors: that we can control or influence**

CHART 2

Cause-and-Effect Planning

Desired Results: _____

Time	Resources: materials, people, equipment, etc.
Strategies: teaching, learning, assessment	**Professional Development**
Expectations of Staff	**Other Factors: that we can control or influence**

CHART 1

Cause-and-Effect Analysis: An Example

Area of Concern: Nonfiction comprehension remains below anticipated results.

Time	Resources: materials, people, equipment, etc.
• Nonfiction reading in primary grades is less than 30% of time. • Nonfiction reading at intermediate level is less than 40% of time.	• No additional nonfiction purchased for students. • Literacy coaches do not have resources.
Strategies: teaching, learning, assessment	**Professional Development**
• Staff know fiction strategies, but toolkit for nonfiction is limited. • Assessments reflect heavy use of fiction.	• No specific time or training is devoted to learning about nonfiction strategies and comprehension.
Expectations of Staff	**Other Factors**
• Staff have not set expectations for students in nonfiction comprehension. • Students are not taught nonfiction strategies in similar way across grades.	• Parents are not given any materials for helping students with nonfiction comprehension. • Take-home books are all fiction.

CHART 2

Cause-and-Effect Planning: An Example

Desired Results: Student nonfiction comprehension scores go up by 25 scale score points on the state assessment.

Time	Resources: materials, people, equipment, etc.
• Increase time for nonfiction reading and comprehension work to 50+% by end of the quarter.	• Allocate money in budget for purchase of nonfiction, leveled reading materials. • Allocate money for nonfiction to support cross-content units. • Allocate resources for a literacy coach.
Strategies: teaching, learning, assessment	**Professional Development**
• Develop a prioritized list of strategies to use across grade levels and content areas after professional development. • Begin revision of assessments to include nonfiction comprehension.	• Send teacher leaders for training in nonfiction strategies. • Do a book study on nonfiction strategies. • Discuss usefulness of strategies and results in professional learning communities.
Expectations of Staff	**Other Factors**
• By the end of the year, develop a new set of expectations for staff and students.	• In time for summer break, develop materials for parents to use with students on nonfiction comprehension.

ANOTHER METHOD FOR CAUSE AND EFFECT: USE A FISHBONE

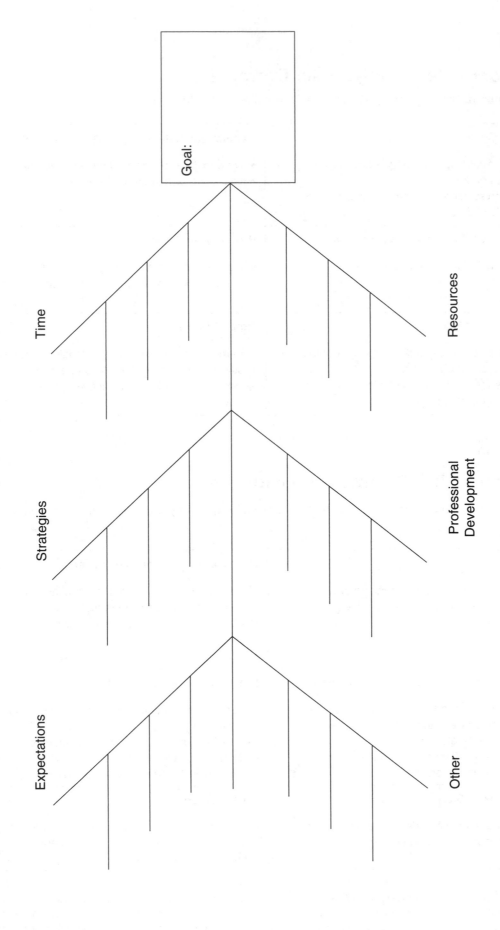

Goal:

Time

Strategies

Expectations

Resources

Professional Development

Other

STRATEGY 49

Celebrations and Next Steps

Purpose: Determining Priorities and Creating Excellence

This technique allows individuals or small groups to use self-reflection and celebration to help determine next steps or priorities for future actions. This method supports and helps sustain efforts by acknowledging accomplishments and building on those successes.

Basics

Number of Participants	Any number
Time Needed	5–30 minutes (variables include size of group, level of depth or complexity)
Room Arrangement	For larger groups, use partners or triads
Difficulty Level	Easy
Brain Bits	Emotional impact and social support and positive feedback
Adult Learning Principle	Experiential: connects to what we know and do well
Materials	Use two sticky notes, a folded piece of paper, or a template
Other	Great for helping teams build on existing and emerging successes; helps reduce "initiative fatigue"

Process Directions

1. Use sticky notes or folded paper and list what we are doing well, what results we are getting, or other celebrations about a particular topic or piece of data.

2. List the area of success.

3. Then be as specific as possible in breaking down the success into components. Cite data sources and list why this success occurred. What factors contributed to the celebrations you listed?

4. Building off what we do well, what are one to three next steps we want to take to expand or sustain our successes? We can also use these steps we took getting to the success as a framework for the next steps we take.

5. Do some whole-group sharing of both parts as examples or post these and read them during a break. After break reflect on a "wow" item that took you by surprise or pleased you.

When

- Use to reinforce hard work.
- Use to note the end of a stressful time or process.
- Use to note results and reinforce what works.
- Use to build off our current successes.

Examples and Uses

1. Math or literacy scores went up as a result of a specific set of actions or processes.
2. Discipline referrals went down due to preventive training such as "Bully Proofing."
3. The parent satisfaction rate increased due to a new telephone and e-mail communication system.
4. Learning teams were successful in helping each teacher acquire at least three new strategies for students who are just learning English.
5. Every student can describe how to correct writing using a model and a scoring guide.

Selected Reference

Gregory and Kuzmich (2004).

BUILD ON SUCCESS!

Area of Success: _____

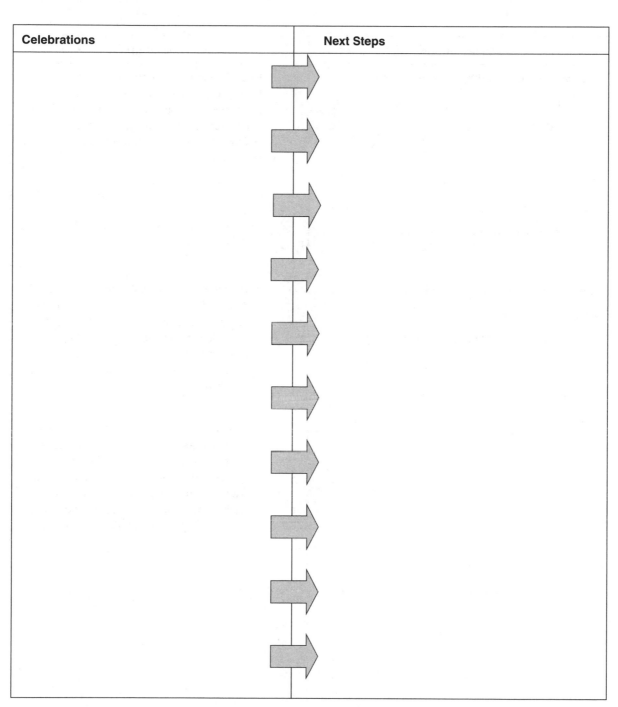

Celebrations	Next Steps

BUILD ON SUCCESS! AN EXAMPLE

Area of Success: Writing Scores Improved

Celebrations	Next Steps
Celebration: Expository writing improved **Data Source:** State and school assessments **Why:** Focus across all content areas Use of common scoring checklist Use of common content-specific model	Every group made progress except for special-education learners: Explore ways for students to transfer skills in writing from special-education setting to other classes. Give more practice at correcting work using color coding.
Celebration: Mechanics improved **Data Sources:** State, district, and school assessments **Why:** Uses of student editing time in every class "Quick" edit strategies practiced in English and reinforced in other classes Extra points given	1. New teachers struggling to fit in editing time and strategies. Pair them with other teachers who are having success and have developed supportive strategies. Give new teachers additional peer coaching time to support school writing initiatives. 2. Mechanics in narrative writing have not improved as much. Replicate the steps used for expository writing, including student editing for homework on narrative pieces of any length and in-class writing. Give extra points and develop and teach quick editing strategies for narrative writing.

STRATEGY 50

Current Snapshot

Purpose: Determining Priorities and Creating Excellence

This method is a great way to sort out what is still important. It is a way to focus and make certain the energy, time, and resources are being directed to fruitful processes and projects.

Basics

Number of Participants	Small groups of 2 to 6 or one large group of no more than 20 to 28
Time Needed	15–30 minutes (varies with size of group)
Room Arrangement	Tables and chairs for small groups or chairs around a chart for large group
Difficulty Level	This method is often humorous and fun The facilitator needs to keep group focused
Brain Bits	Emotional impact and social support, development of common understanding
Adult Learning Principle	Experiential: connects to what we know and do well Life application: If I need to implement it, it should be worth my time
Materials	Template or wall chart and sticky notes
Other	Several ways to do this: Peterson and Deal (2002) suggest a "taking out the garbage method" that has the same purpose. See second example at end of this section

Process Directions

1. Introduce the template or wall chart and the purpose.

2. Each participant adds to one section of the template or wall chart at a time. Repeat five times for each section. If you use a wall chart, have participants put responses on sticky notes.

3. Process the activity by discussing the focus of time, resources, materials, and people toward the "seeds, beds, and full flowers."

When

- This is a great beginning-of-the-year activity when we have new staff or team members.
- Staff or team members feel overwhelmed.

- We want to target limited resources in the right direction
- We need to tell the story of where we have been and where we are going so that the target and journey are easily understood by all

Examples and Uses

1. We need to get the picture of what we have done in math and why.

2. Use to review the complete list of work we have put into incentives for secondary students to give their best efforts on assessments.

3. Use to assess professional development in writing: what helped us increase student achievement and what did not.

4. Use to evaluate use of a program or materials and what impact parts of the total program had on students.

Selected References

Bailey (1995), Chadwick (2006), Chang and Dalziel (1999b), Gregory and Kuzmich (2004), Roberts and Pruitt (2003), Wald and Castleberry (2000).

CURRENT SNAPSHOT

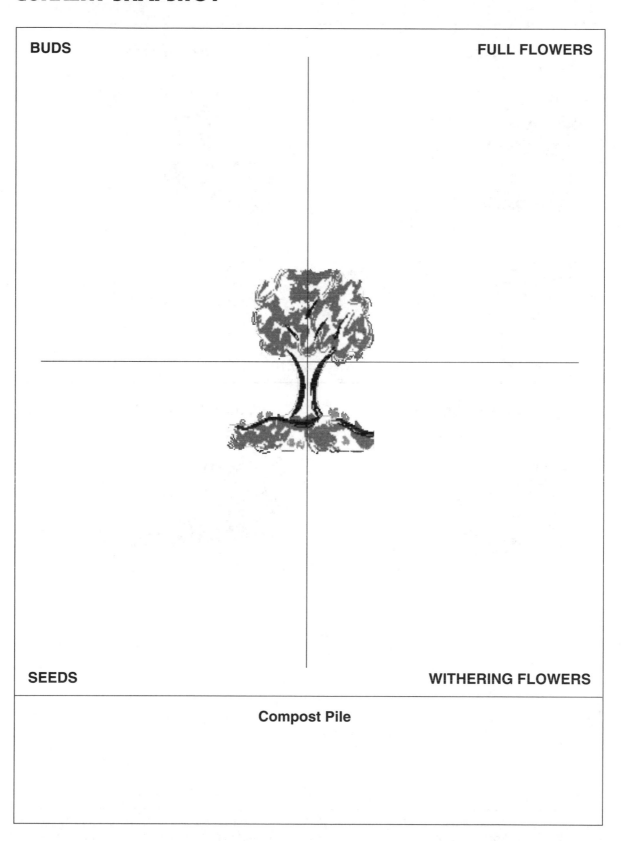

BUDS

FULL FLOWERS

SEEDS

WITHERING FLOWERS

Compost Pile

TAKING OUT THE TRASH

Keep This!	Store This!
Garage Sale This!	**Toxic Waste Removal!**

STRATEGY 51

Four Squares for Creativity

Purpose: Determining Priorities and Creating Excellence

This method helps groups or individuals prioritize work, look at ideas or issues from a new angle, expand the possibilities or solutions to a problem, and analyze the impact of possible solutions. The focus on creativity helps adults rejuvenate thinking and increases the probability of success.

Basics

Number of Participants	Works well with one to four people; two to three is ideal
Time Needed	15–30 minutes (depending on complexity of the topic or issue)
Room Arrangement	Opportunity to work quietly with a few people at a table or in any small-group arrangement
Difficulty Level	This is a good activity to do with established groups that have had other opportunities to interact Directions should be given with an example discussed or modeled
Brain Bits	This process emphasizes the reflective learning system; adults reflect better when given the opportunity to ask questions and analyze a topic deeply. Process supports social and active learning and gives adults access to new ideas and a chance to integrate the new learning with the old
Adult Learning Principle	Experiential: so that connections from new learning to old are clear, opportunities to prioritize work are provided, and there is time for reflection
Materials	Time for groups to work, template provided, directions given with modeling or a written model
Other	This is a great method for understanding items from a brainstormed list more deeply. It is a great method for comparing the viability of a variety of solutions quickly

Process Directions

1. Review the purpose for this activity in terms of establishing priority and looking at the problem, issue, or topic from a new perspective.

2. Model the process using a well-understood issue such as assessment results and challenges, the decision-making process and its effectiveness, a process like six-trait writing or problem-based math, or behavioral expectations.

3. Brainstorm aspects of the problem or process in questions such as contributing factors or possible solutions.

4. Ask each small group to select one aspect from the brainstormed list.

5. Use the template to fully think through the issue or topic selected.

6. Share one or more four squares with total group if you have six or fewer small groups. With more small groups, pair groups after the templates are complete and share. Ask these groups to share common viewpoints.

7. Gather templates and use to report back on priorities for next steps or possible viewpoints that further the solution to a problem.

When

- Use when setting priorities.
- Use when determining which solutions to a problem a team should pursue.
- Data are stagnant and new points of view may help a group get "unstuck" with regard to the results or methods used currently.
- Use to reminding staff or parents what steps in a process mean to the group.

Examples and Uses

1. After analyzing summative data and listing challenges, this method may help develop better solutions or help analyze the viability of each solution.

2. Use with an issue at your school that involves a complex process or procedure list such as discipline or decision making to improve the process or update common understandings.

3. Use when people have multiple initiatives proposed to help others see the possibilities for prioritizing the initiatives.

Selected References

Gregory and Kuzmich (2005a, 2005b), Renzulli (1994), Torrance (1998).

FOUR SQUARES FOR CREATIVITY

Topic: _____

List as many facts or things you know about the topic as you can in five minutes. Include your data sources. Use brainstorming rules.	How would other people feel about this topic? You can guess.
Fluency	*Flexibility*
Originality	*Elaboration*
1. Think of a new point of view about the topic. 2. Develop a name or title for your point of view. _____ 3. What will it help us do or think? _____ _____ 4. Draw a symbol for your point of view or new idea:	Describe your point of view or new idea as if it were an advertisement or editorial on the Internet or in the newspaper. Give it a level of importance or priority.

SOURCE: From Gregory and Kuzmich (2005b).

FOUR SQUARES FOR CREATIVITY: AN EXAMPLE

List as many facts or things you know about the topic as you can in five minutes. Include your data sources. Use brainstorming rules.

State, district, and classroom assessments:

- Importance in inferential thinking
- Importance in creating meaning
- Content-specific vocabulary
- From professional development
- Strategies that promote practice and use of vocabulary
- Meaningful repetition
- Use in reading, writing, speaking, and listening

Fluency

How would other people feel about this topic? You can guess.

- Not certain what methods work best
- What methods or strategies work in which content areas?
- Why students don't remember vocabulary from one day to the next
- The relationship of nonfiction and vocabulary acquisition

Flexibility

Originality

1. Think of a new point of view about the topic. *How do successfully literate students learn vocabulary?*

2. Name your point of view. *Student-Proven Strategies*

3. What will it help us do or think? *Looking at what successful students do helps teachers use and select strategies that engage other students who may struggle. It helps us form a basic toolkit of strategies for students that we can add to if needed, for struggling students.*

4. Draw a symbol for your point of view or new idea:

Elaboration

Describe your point of view or new idea as if it were an advertisement or editorial on the Internet or in the newspaper. Give it a level of importance or priority.

Four Proven Strategies for All Students

This is a very high priority for our school and our team. Vocabulary is one of the five major components of functional literacy and is the cornerstone of understanding content-area ideas.

STRATEGY 52

Lesson and Unit Studies

Purpose: Determining Priorities and Creating Excellence

Lesson studies have been widely researched starting in Japan, and now in this country, and are the source of research at regional laboratories and other facilities. Results using these types of methods are dramatic. Just as with examining student work, the questions we ask about such studies can help us get further faster. Since numerous protocols already exist, we focus this strategy on asking the right questions before, during, and after the lesson or unit study.

Basics

Number of Participants	Small groups or partners
Time Needed	30 minutes to one hour to set up, classroom observation time, debrief of one or more hours
Room Arrangement	Small groups
Difficulty Level	Difficult and high risk
Brain Bits	People need social relationships that validate and result in acceptance. We need to use "sense-making" actions to move forward in our learning. People need trustworthy environments in which to work and grow
Adult Learning Principle	Adults need to connect to what we do well, see the real-life use in learning, and have their unique circumstances acknowledged
Materials	Lesson or unit plans Chart paper Notecards or journal entries
Other	It is best to use this strategy with an established group that has a high degree of trust. Start with more veteran staff to model for newer staff. Send small groups into the classroom or even one other peer coach

Process Directions

1. Start with a study of existing curriculum and standards. Teachers can identify and discuss larger and critical concepts and skills to be demonstrated by students.

2. Choose a lesson within the context of a larger unit. Review the unit plan to determine the match to the standards and curriculum as well as the desired student demonstration

of thinking and other skills. Discuss how the lesson to be observed fits in the overall unit plan. Discuss how this lesson will contribute to the students' performance on the final assessment for the unit.

3. Observe in the classroom by collecting data on student thinking and the rigor of the lesson, teacher strategy selection for instruction and for student learning, and leverage in the lesson that will help students generalize and utilize skills learned in future known and unknown contexts.

4. Use a cause-and-effect format to debrief the lesson. Guide the teacher observed through the thinking and then use a tuning or other protocol to help the group process the lesson and make suggestions.

5. The group helps the teacher plan for the next lesson based on learning from colleagues' review of the lesson observed. Sometimes two or three cycles of observation really help teachers make the growth with students, which is the desired result of lesson studies. Repeat the process for the current teacher or repeat the process for the next teacher in the group.

When

- Use with established groups where climate and culture is excellent.
- Use with groups of teachers who want to accelerate the growth of students rapidly.
- Use with teachers who are struggling with aspects of learning and teaching and want peer assistance to determine the best solutions.
- Use as job-embedded coaching method for peers.

Examples and Uses

1. Teachers are struggling with differentiation management or implementation in their classrooms.

2. A particular group of students such as English-Language Learners, gifted learners, or special-education students is not making sufficient or rapid growth.

3. Teachers are challenged by the need to raise the level of both rigor and relevance in their instruction.

4. Student motivation needs improvement or student completion of tasks at a high-quality level needs to improve.

Selected References

Columbia University, Teachers College Lesson Study Research Group (2005); Lewis (2002, 2003, 2005); Richardson (2000/2001, 2004).

BEFORE THE LESSON OBSERVATION

This is a good idea for reviewing curriculum and standards, as well as the unit plan, assessment, and lesson to be observed.

DO A WEB TALK

The teacher webs the upcoming lesson, detailing the critical concepts and their relationship to the standards, assessment, and curriculum.

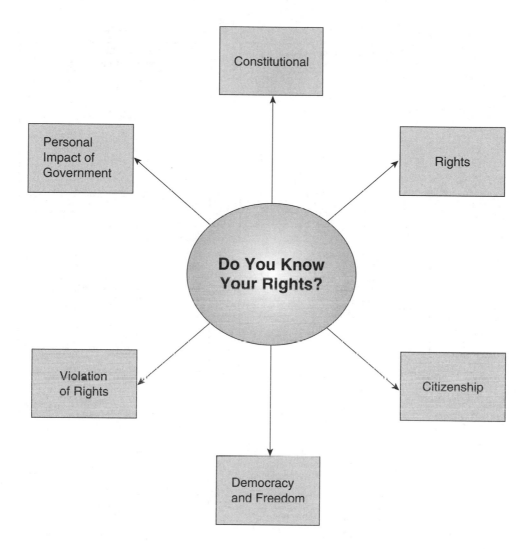

SOURCE: Gregory and Kuzmich (2004).

IDEA FOR OBSERVING IN THE CLASSROOM OF A FELLOW TEACHER

Use a journaling method of recording data.

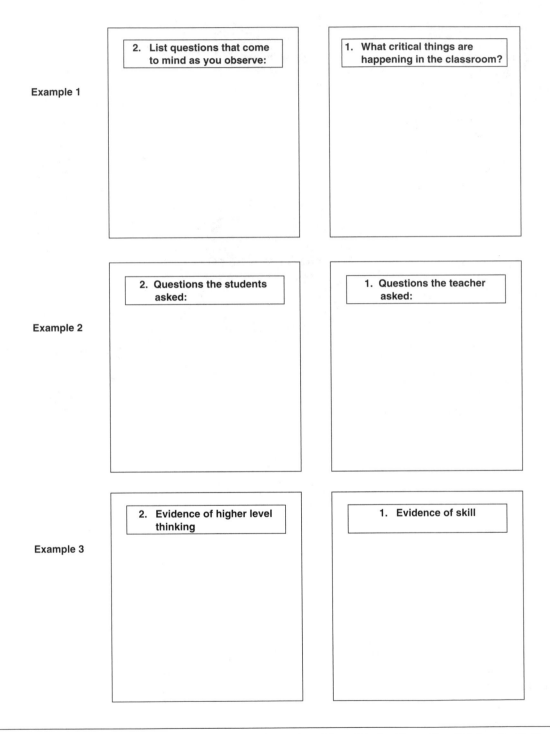

Example 1

> 2. List questions that come to mind as you observe:

> 1. What critical things are happening in the classroom?

Example 2

> 2. Questions the students asked:

> 1. Questions the teacher asked:

Example 3

> 2. Evidence of higher level thinking

> 1. Evidence of skill

Processing Method for After the Lesson

Use a Form of Stepped Reflection and Planning

Teacher reflects on whether the lesson produced the intended results and evidence of those results.

Group of observers:

1. Each takes turns commenting on his or her notes and observations.

2. Each asks teacher questions.

3. Each reflects on teacher's answers.

4. Each makes suggestions.

Teacher and Group:

1. Web next lesson and add suggested strategies.

2. List "look fors" with the teacher in terms of student learning.

3. Discuss what success will or should look like in the next lesson.

4. Discuss what the most effective feedback will be for the teacher. The teacher designs the journal or note-taking tool.

5. Plan to meet and repeat the Stepped Reflection and Planning process.

STRATEGY 53

Prioritizing the Impact of Solutions

Purpose: Determining Priorities and Creating Excellence

This is a great method of helping staff prioritize solutions. Using a cross-impact matrix such as this helps staff weigh the difficulties and potential payoff of solutions. It might help staff start with solutions that have low difficulty and high impact and then work their way toward the higher difficulty items, depending on the impact for students.

Basics

Number of Participants	Small and larger groups depending on process time
Time Needed	It takes about 8 to 10 minutes to place each solution on the matrix and discuss it. With five possible solutions, the process could take from 45–50 minutes
Room Arrangement	Tables for group work and chairs
Difficulty Level	Low risk
Brain Bits	Supports emotional and social needs, needs for prioritization, and needs to establish common vocabulary
Adult Learning Principle	Choice and prioritization, opportunity for reflection, transferable work
Materials	Large chart with matrix, sticky notes, markers, pens, tape
Other	Before the meeting, have people rank the solutions in terms of importance for students (send solutions out ahead for consideration). Rank again for the amount of resources, time, and personnel to pull them off

Process Directions

1. Put the matrix up on the wall and explain the process.

2. Put each solution on a sticky note or card that can be easily read by participants. The more people, the larger the display needs to be for visibility.

3. Discuss ranking for impact on students. Facilitate for tentative agreement and place along the impact line.

4. Discuss the rankings for difficulty in terms of resources, time, and personnel; move solution cards or notes to the right quadrant. The solution should now be ranked according to both the difficulty and the impact.

5. Discuss which solutions to start with. Rank the solutions with the highest student impact and least difficulty to tackle first.

6. Create follow-up with an action plan for one or two of the solutions or strategies. This could be done by a small team of three or four and sent out to the rest for verification and refinement.

When

- The number of tasks or amount of work seems overwhelming.
- Use prior to action planning for the school year.
- You need to verify assumptions about difficulty about four to eight weeks after the action plan is in place. Some solutions look easier at first than actual experience shows.

Examples and Uses

1. Staff see the need to improve math scores and want to tackle curriculum and assessment design, strategies acquisition, and new material implementation all at once. This lack of focus can overwhelm any initiative.

2. Parents are dissatisfied with the progress and services for gifted learners and solutions are numerous.

3. Staff brainstormed an excellent list of 15 ideas to combat tardiness or absences.

Selected References

Ambrose (2002), Gordon and Hayward (1968).

PRIORITIZING THE IMPACT OF SOLUTIONS

Difficulty level = Time, resources, skills, expectations/attitudes, people

Impact level = The effect of an activity, action, task, or project reaching the goal (probability of reaching your desired result)

You can plot solutions on a grid that looks like this

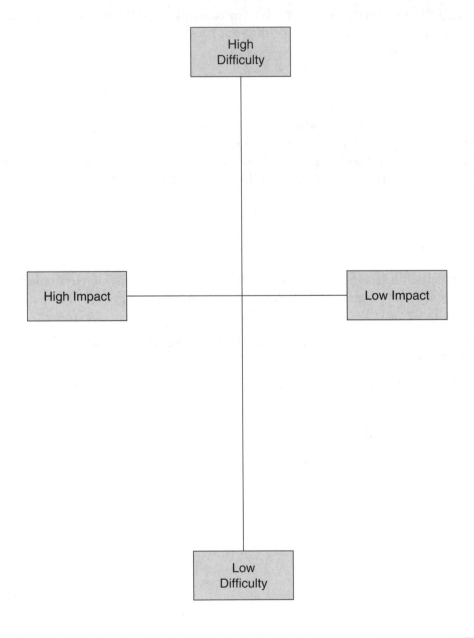

STRATEGY 54

Prioritizing Work and Learning

Purpose: Determining Priorities and Creating Excellence

Planning for results can be done in many formats. Creating easily understood documentation that details the order and priority of the work helps staff and community members better support the effort it takes to create excellence for our students.

Basics

Number of Participants	Small groups organized by topic or goal area
Time Needed	Two sessions of approximately 60 minutes
Room Arrangement	Small tables with no more than six people per group and no less than three people
Difficulty Level	Low risk for established teams, takes some time but not difficult
Brain Bits	Develops cognitive learning in terms of developing common vocabulary and optimizes positive influences of team
Adult Learning Principle	Self-directed: Adults need choice and opportunities to prioritize their work Life application: determine real-life use and process of transfer to participants' unique circumstances
Materials	Planning guide on paper or chart, markers, tape, sticky notes
Other	It helps to use the template once as a total group to show how previously accomplished work or work already under way would look in this format If the tasks or actions are too complex to fit in the template, they need to be adjusted and be broken down further to become more attainable in a reasonable amount of time

Process Directions

1. First determine the two or three measurable goals or critical questions to answer for the year through other processes such as "KWL," "Probable and Preferred Future," or other goal-setting methods.

2. List the tasks on sticky notes or other movable pieces of paper.

3. Put the tasks in order of importance (payoff for students) or logical sequence.

4. Now list what actions must be done to accomplish the steps and put them in order.

5. Finally, add a "who and when" component to finish this portion of the plan.

6. Also, include an opportunity to reflect on and celebrate the completion of each portion of the plan. This also allows adjustments to be made to alter timing or other resources.

When

- This process is a great next step after a team or school decides upon one or two measurable goals for the year. The plan is designed to describe the work to be accomplished this year or over a two-year period.
- This process also works well to help small professional learning communities prioritize the work for the next few months or portion of the year.

Examples and Uses

1. Each team at a middle-level school designs a process for reducing bullying incidents.

2. Small groups at an elementary school decide how to implement two or three vocabulary or writing strategies.

3. High school teams, either by department or cross-disciplinary teams, reflect on the use of "accessible text" strategies.

4. Teams focus on gathering and determining anchor papers and writing samples for use with students.

5. Parent groups use this process to plan an event or fundraiser.

6. Professional learning communities have developed a question or answer or a specific goal and need a planning method.

Selected References

Ambrose (2002), Gordon (1961), Mind Tools (2006a, 2006b, 2006c), Roukes (1988), Wald and Castleberry (2000).

PLANNING TEMPLATE FOR PRIORITIZING WORK AND LEARNING

Goal or critical question to answer (specific, achievable in timeframe, and measurable where possible):

_____

_____

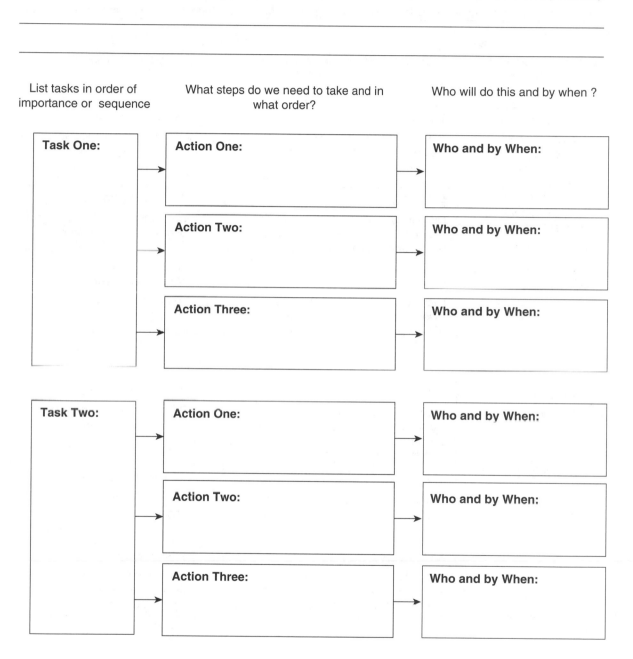

List tasks in order of importance or sequence	What steps do we need to take and in what order?	Who will do this and by when ?
Task One:	**Action One:**	**Who and by When:**
	Action Two:	**Who and by When:**
	Action Three:	**Who and by When:**
Task Two:	**Action One:**	**Who and by When:**
	Action Two:	**Who and by When:**
	Action Three:	**Who and by When:**

PLANNING TEMPLATE FOR PRIORITIZING WORK AND LEARNING: AN EXAMPLE

Goal or critical question to answer:

Improve inferential thinking in expository text by getting 15% more of our students to proficient or higher levels by next year.

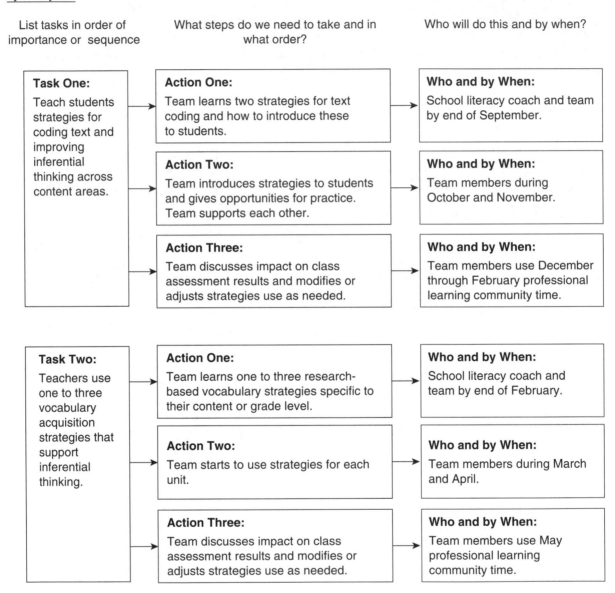

List tasks in order of importance or sequence

What steps do we need to take and in what order?

Who will do this and by when?

Task One:

Teach students strategies for coding text and improving inferential thinking across content areas.

Action One:

Team learns two strategies for text coding and how to introduce these to students.

Who and by When:

School literacy coach and team by end of September.

Action Two:

Team introduces strategies to students and gives opportunities for practice. Team supports each other.

Who and by When:

Team members during October and November.

Action Three:

Team discusses impact on class assessment results and modifies or adjusts strategies use as needed.

Who and by When:

Team members use December through February professional learning community time.

Task Two:

Teachers use one to three vocabulary acquisition strategies that support inferential thinking.

Action One:

Team learns one to three research-based vocabulary strategies specific to their content or grade level.

Who and by When:

School literacy coach and team by end of February.

Action Two:

Team starts to use strategies for each unit.

Who and by When:

Team members during March and April.

Action Three:

Team discusses impact on class assessment results and modifies or adjusts strategies use as needed.

Who and by When:

Team members use May professional learning community time.

STRATEGY 55

Probable and Preferred Future

Purpose: Determining Priorities and Creating Excellence

This process is designed to unify a group around common priorities for future action. It also helps groups deal with worry about problems or causes and move to a solution orientation.

Basics

Number of Participants	Small groups of 3 to 8, or large group of no more than 20
Time Needed	Small groups will need 30–45 minutes Large group will need approximately one hour This method requires some review by individuals and then a follow-up meeting of about 30 minutes to complete the process
Room Arrangement	Small groups: around wall areas Large group: near a large wall area
Difficulty Level	This activity is not difficult when used for prioritizing solutions This activity requires careful facilitation if used to move from blame and causes to focus on solutions. Steps of the protocol should help with this. The facilitator will need to keep individuals from dominating the group or stopping the forward progress of the work While this process takes time, the buy-in from staff that results is well worth it
Brain Bits	This is certainly an activity that supports social and emotional validation needs of adults. Putting work in context and making personal connections is essential to adult analysis and acceptances

(Continued)

(Continued)

Adult Learning Principles	Experiential: adults need to connect to new ideas
	Self-directed: adults need choice and to prioritize work tasks
	Opportunities for reflection in times of change are essential
Materials	Markers, roll of chart paper at least 4 × 16 or four sheets of chart paper per group, tape
Other	Be certain to review the directions for each step and give examples if needed
	Allow plenty of time to move from the first step to subsequent steps
	Keep flow of discussion focused with turns for all participants if the topics are controversial

Process Directions

1. The facilitator prepares a large wall chart with four columns or four pieces of chart paper: "Current Conditions," "Probable Future," "Preferred Future," and "Action Plan for Change."

2. The facilitator asks staff members: "Think about the current state of . . . in your . . . (school, your state, and the nation)." List details about the current state of a particular issue including results, data sources, and supporting details.

3. Ask staff: "If the current trends continue, what is the probable future scenario or result?" A "Think, Pair, Share" method works well for this step. Individuals think by writing a few thoughts down and sharing with a partner and then the group.

4. The facilitator asks staff what they would prefer to have happen for the future of the team, school, students, and so forth. List ideas once and add wording as participants duplicate ideas to honor different versions. The facilitator may need to remind participants to list what they can control and influence versus broad wishes for general groups.

5. Based on the information in the previous column, the next activity is to generate actions and solutions that would move the staff toward the "Preferred Future." Use the following approach: Write ideas on sticky notes and bring them up to that chart. Take a brief break and have two or three staff members group ideas into categories. Report on this at the end of the brief break. Set a team in place to refine the ideas and combine them.

6. Put the final action plan out to staff with a request to review for the next meeting. At that meeting, further refine the ideas. Then prioritize the steps through discussion. Keeping in mind the difficulty and the impact on students helps most groups prioritize more easily.

Selected References

Albright and Shaller (1998), Bailey (1995), Garcia and Bray (1997), Wald and Castleberry (2000).

PROBABLE AND PREFERRED FUTURE

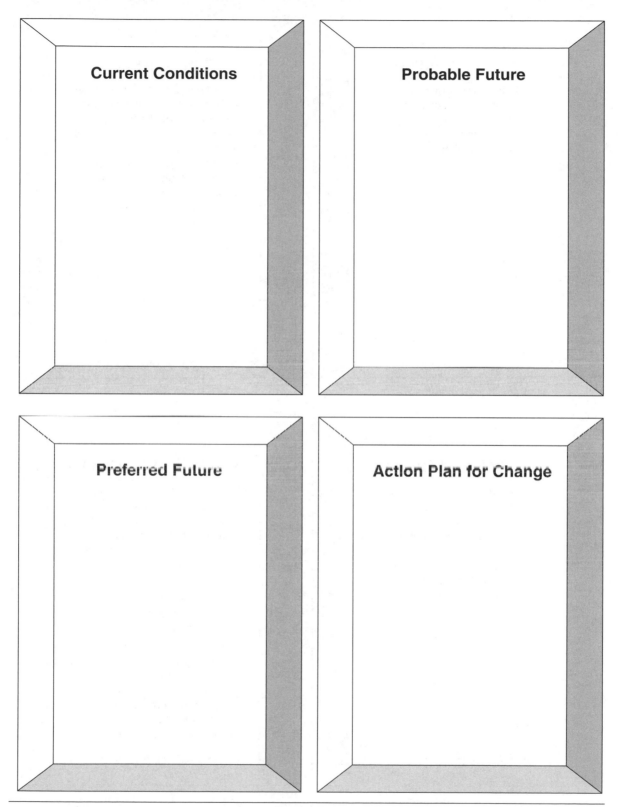

| Current Conditions | Probable Future |

| Preferred Future | Action Plan for Change |

PROBABLE AND PREFERRED FUTURE: AN EXAMPLE

Current Conditions

Math scores remain low and static, especially in problem solving, numeracy, pattern recognition, and statistics and probability.

Probable Future

If we keep the same curriculum, materials, and strategies, our results will not change. The progress in reading and writing in math is helping subtest scores in algebraic concepts and has resulted in a slight change in problem solving for some subgroups. This trend may continue.

Preferred Future

All subgroups improve in all six math standards on state and national assessments.

We will accelerate the progress of students who are further behind while ensuring the growth of those at or above Proficient within the next three years.

Action Plan for Change

1. Do a thorough curriculum and assessment audit to determine critical or power standards; adjust and align expectations and demonstrations of skill within the next six months.

2. Explore materials and resources to match new alignment within the six months after the alignment.

3. Next year, focus efforts on training for planning with new assessments and curriculum and follow-up time to explore appropriate research-based strategies that support modern math instruction.

STRATEGY 56

Pros and Cons

Purpose: Building Resilience and Creating Solutions

This is a great process for sorting solutions and making decisions. Understanding the pros and cons and advantages and disadvantages all help to select the best solutions. Anticipating any roadblocks or issues is necessary to keep the momentum of any project in place. This method also helps a group get unstuck.

Basics

Number of Participants	Small group of two or more
Time Needed	Depends on the number of solutions or strategies being considered, usually takes 5–8 minutes per solution
Room Arrangement	Small table groups
Difficulty Level	Moderate level of difficulty; any time multiple points of view are at issue, time for processing and staying on task will be critical
Brain Bits	Adults need to sort and prioritize to make sense of the work or learning. Emotional needs of participants are dealt with through processes that respect experiences and multiple points of view
Adult Learning Principle	Adults like experiential learning and ample opportunity to reflect when tasks will impact them
Materials	Template or charts and markers

Process Directions

1. Given a problem or goal that a group is going to tackle, use any of the brainstorming techniques to develop a list of possible solutions.

2. Take each of the solutions and analyze them as to the following:
   a. Pros and cons
   b. Pluses and minuses (use instead of pros and cons if desired)
   c. Advantages and disadvantages
   d. Benefits and hindrances

3. Discuss which solutions have benefits that outweigh negative or roadblock issues. These are the solutions the group can incorporate at the start of its planning.

When

- Use to prioritize solutions.
- Use to remove roadblocks.

- Use to get a group unstuck.
- Use to know where to start on a complex or multifaceted project.
- Use to assist with shared decision making.

Examples and Uses

1. A math group has several strategies for improving problem solving and wants to figure out which one to start with or which one might have the highest payoff.

2. A community group is trying to learn about Internet access abuses and the solutions to this problem. The members want to weigh the solutions against the impact on student learning.

3. Literacy learning teams are trying to prioritize the use of the literacy coach's time. Several solutions have been proposed.

Selected References

Beaudoin and Taylor (2004); Burke (1993); Chadwick (2006); Chang and Buster (1999); Costa and Garmston (2002); Daniels (1986); Deal and Peterson (1998, 2002); Johnson, Johnson, and Smith (1991b); Roberts and Pruitt (2003).

PROS AND CONS

Template Ideas

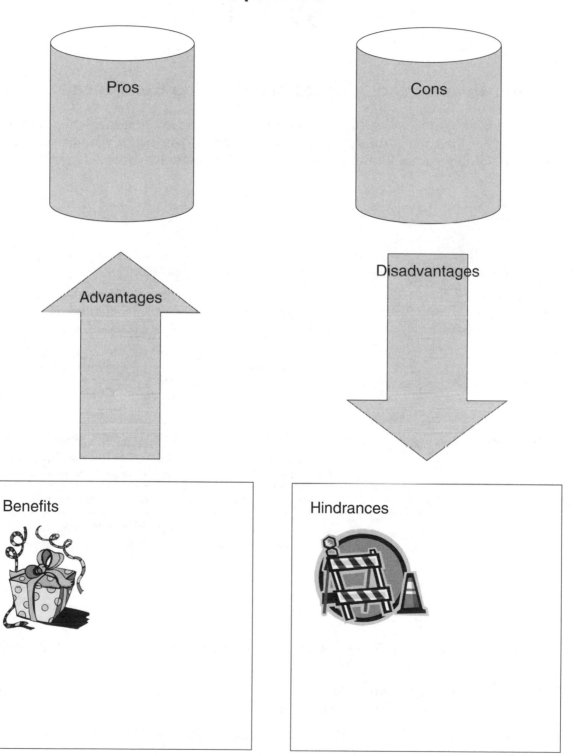

STRATEGY 57

SWOT

Purpose: Determining Priorities and Creating Excellence

This activity is a great way to "take stock" before starting new projects, when completing tasks, or when the momentum gets slowed or stopped. This activity makes certain any potential roadblocks are acknowledged and dealt with before they interfere with progress.

Basics

Number of Participants	Small groups of two to eight
Time Needed	20–30 minutes (varies with number of people)
Room Arrangement	Tables and chairs
Difficulty Level	Average risk; facilitator needs to keep the focus on what we can accomplish and removal of roadblocks
Brain Bits	Support the need for common language, emotional and social connections
Adult Learning Principle	Experiential: connects to what we know and do well Life application: determine real-life use and process of transfer to participants' unique circumstances
Materials	Use template or create responses on chart paper
Other	This process helps put problems or issues in perspective and reaffirm what we *can* get done

Process Directions

1. Introduce the idea of SWOT (strengths, weaknesses, opportunities, and threats) and explain the reasons and purpose for its use.

2. Start by listing strengths related to an issue, goal, or problem. Ask: What do we do well? What strengths do our people have now?

3. Then list weaknesses. Ask: Where do we need to improve? What skills are not yet in place?

4. Third, list opportunities we may have, such as a grant, new technology, training, or other resources, events, and people to help us. Ask: What are interesting trends do we know about? What advantages and resources do we have in place?

5. Finally, list any threats to our success. Ask: What obstacles do we face? What should we avoid? What roadblocks might get in our way?

6. A good follow-up discussion should be about how to avoid limits or remove such threats so that the progress and work of the group can continue.

When

- This is a good tool for refocusing a group.
- Use when dealing roadblocks or stalled momentum.
- Multiple points of view need to be acknowledged.
- Use when starting a major project or checking on progress.

Examples and Uses

1. Use to determine the impact of a solution for increased parent involvement.

2. Use to determine the plausibility of a solution for closing the achievement gap.

3. Use when starting a new initiative in math.

4. Use to evaluate the effectiveness of professional development opportunity.

5. Use to revisit a school improvement plan.

Selected References

Chapman (2005); Dosher, Benepe, Humphrey, Stewart, and Lie (1960–1970).

SWOT

Issue and Topic:

Strengths:

Weaknesses:

Opportunities:

Threats:

SWOT: AN EXAMPLE

Issue and Topic:

We want to create and sustain professional learning communities at our school to further the progress toward increased student achievement.

Strengths:

- Use of in-house experts
- Time planned for early release each week
- Time to get good at sharing and helping each other
- A wealth of great ideas among staff members
- Group problem solving for better solutions
- Dividing up the work

Weaknesses:

- We need to learn strategies to organize, run, and sustain our professional learning communities
- Our facilitators do not have leadership and facilitation training yet
- We don't have a clear understanding of what the professional learning communities can do

Opportunities:

- Ability to organize by different jobs, alike and diverse teams
- Use of electronic folders to share proven strategies and ideas
- Time to plan and develop solutions

Threats:

- Parent perception of early release time
- Worry about not meeting adequate yearly progress and the associated consequences
- Worry that this is just one more initiative that will be difficult to sustain

STRATEGY 58

The Interview

Purpose: Determining Priorities and Creating Excellence

Going to the source and interviewing stakeholders is an excellent way to help a team focus and develop creative solutions. Using an interview to help charge the team or reinvent a solution is a great way to fine-tune the work and keep a strong focus on the desired results.

Basics

Number of Participants	Any
Time Needed	15–25 minutes
Room Arrangement	Any facing the interviewee
Difficulty Level	Medium to high risk
Brain Bits	Reflective learning is a key to adult processing; adults reflect better when given the opportunity to ask questions and analyze a topic of data deeply This process supports social learning and gives adults access to new ideas or an opportunity to see ideas from the viewpoints of others
Adult Learning Principle	Experiential: so that connections from new learning to old are clear, opportunities to prioritize work are provided, and there is time for reflection
Materials	Depending on the size of the venue, microphones may be necessary—one for interviewee and one to pass around to team members. For small groups, only seating furnishings are needed
Other	Gathering the recipients of your work or ideas and confirming the direction is a powerful tool for prioritization and creativity

Process Directions

1. Identify a major roadblock or a fork in the road with your plan for improvement.

2. At that point, invite in one to three stakeholders: those who will benefit from, receive, or need to contribute to the work.

3. Orient the interviewees to the work being done before the interview. Also give them a few starting points or questions to answer.

4. The facilitator starts the interview with a prompt from the questions or points given to the interviewee ahead of time and lets the interviewee respond. Give this about 5 to 10 minutes.

5. Invite the rest of the team members to ask the interviewee follow-up questions for about 10 to 15 minutes.

6. After the interviewee leaves, process what you have learned. Use "Plus, Minus, Interesting," "3-2-1," or any other conversation starters that allow individual reflection first and then group processing. Decide how what you learned will influence the next steps of your work.

When

- A team is stuck.
- A team has too long a list of "to do's".
- A team needs a creative boost to problem solving or solution creation.
- Use to reorient the group to the purpose of the work or the desired result.
- Use as a celebration of success.

Examples and Uses

1. A team manages to boost math scores. Three students who were successful are invited in. The students may be at various performance levels; however, all have shown growth. Ask students what strategies had the greatest payoff, and what they are the most proud of in their math gains. This is a great way to celebrate and move the team to next steps in the work.

2. A high school team is restructuring the ninth-grade year. Several students are interviewed: some who dropped out, some who stayed and turned around some tough times, and some who met with success. This interview will help the team know where to start and how to prioritize steps that help students when they reach a fork in the road to success.

3. An elementary team is trying to increase parent involvement. Several parents are brought in or home visits are conducted using the same questions. This will help the team choose the best solutions that make parents feel welcome and involved.

4. Interview new teachers at the end of the year to determine what supports worked and what was lacking. This will help a district or school structure new-teacher support for maximum success or even differentiate the support by need or experience. This may also help a team plan for second- and third-year follow-up support.

5. Videotape interviews of students or other stakeholders as a regular part of data collection for the school or program. Use this to help plan next steps and assess the success of initiatives.

Selected Reference

National School Board Association (2005).

SAMPLE INTERVIEW QUESTIONS

Students

1. What were your biggest successes, and what were your challenges?

2. What could we do differently to help you be more successful?

3. When you reached the point where you had to change your behaviors and experiences, what happened at school or home that helped you the most?

4. What are your favorite strategies that work for you in . . . (list content area or skill)?

5. What do you want us to know as we plan for . . . (list initiative)?

6. What could we do differently to support our students?

7. What really helped you learn . . . (English, math, etc.)?

Parents

1. How could we make our school and staff more welcoming?

2. What do you need to know about your student to help you help your child?

3. How can we support you and your family?

4. What would make your experience with our school better or more positive?

5. What is something we could have done differently for you or your student and why? What should we have done?

6. How is our communication to you and your family? What method works best for you: notes, e-mail, Web site, phone, and so forth?

7. What aspects of our school are the most confusing? What processes are the clearest?

Other Staff Members

1. What support do you need with . . . (list initiative)?

2. What is the greatest need you have, and what kind of support do you suggest?

3. Which populations of students are the most challenging? Why? What would help you better meet the needs of these students?

4. How difficult is it to communicate with the parents of your students? What would help you?

5. Do you know how decisions get made at this school or district? Do you participate? What would make this process work better?

6. What kind of training format works best for you (workshops, coaching, video, book studies, student work analysis, lesson study, data review, cooperative planning, etc.)?

7. As an expert in your content area or grade level, what is the best advice you can give us for improving student achievement? Meeting diverse student needs? Choosing the strategies to teach new teachers? Sharing the practices that have the highest payoff for students?

8. What could we do to help you feel part of the process? A valued member of our team, school, or district? Better informed? More supported? What could we do to help you get access to the right resources to do your work?

Interview Follow-up Ideas

1. What surprised you? Tell a partner; now share with the whole group.

2. What did you learn that should guide our work? List the two most important things on the chart near your table.

3. Did anything you learn change your mind about our priorities, the direction in which we are heading, or the solutions we have chosen?

4. What else do you need to know to move our work forward? Who else do we need to hear from?

5. What struck you as the most powerful thing an interviewee said today? How will this influence your thinking and beliefs about our work?

STRATEGY 59

The People Ladder

Purpose: Determining Priorities and Creating Excellence

The "People Ladder" is an interactive activity to determine the importance of a set of actions, plans, strategies, or solutions developed to address a goal or problem. Staff must organize and prioritize these solutions or strategies to reflect the best results for students given an agreed-upon criteria.

Basics

Number of Participants	Small groups create criteria for excellence. The large group or small groups can do the People Ladder
Time Needed	20–40 minutes (depends on size of group)
Room Arrangement	Sufficient floor space to stand near a ladder; small groups need tables and chairs
Difficulty Level	Lower risk, two-part activity
Brain Bits	Emotional impact and social support, development of cognitive learning in terms of developing common vocabulary, movement suits our need for physical interaction
Adult Learning Principle	Experiential: connects to what we know and do well Life application: determine real-life use and process of transfer to participants' unique circumstances
Materials	Writing materials at tables, charts, a ladder about five to six feet minimum that can lay flat on the floor, markers, tape
Other	You can do this activity without an actual ladder, or you can make a vertical ladder on the wall with tape and give participants dots to rank priorities and solutions. For the wall version, use a different-color dot for each issue, strategy, or solution

Process Directions

1. Start with a goal or problem that the staff is going to work on this year. The facilitator will have staff brainstorm a list of solutions or strategies about this issue or goal. Ask participants to put solutions or strategies on sticky notes.

2. Select a small group of three to four and sort the sticky notes into groups. Develop headings for those groups or big ideas to label the solutions and strategies.

3. Explain that the People Ladder will help participants prioritize the strategies and solutions. First, however, you will need criteria to decide where to put each solution along the ladder. Strategies placed lower are less of a priority, and strategies placed higher are critical to the success of this work.

4. Start creating these criteria by facilitating a conversation about what excellence for students looks like given the goal or problem. So, if we do a great job meeting this goal, what will it look like? How will students benefit? Each small group offers one idea. Write the items on a chart paper large enough for all to see. The facilitator can encourage staff to add any other critical items at the end. Do not duplicate items.

5. Ask participants to read down the list for excellence when considering each solution or strategy.
   - If the solution meets only a few of the criteria for excellence, they will need to move the solution low on the ladder.
   - If the solution or strategy meets some of the criteria, they will need to place the solution at the middle of the ladder.
   - If the strategy meets most or all of the criteria, it should be placed high on the ladder.
   - Doing this will help prioritize or sequence properly given the usual constraints on time and resources.

6. Bring up a representative group of 8 to 12 staff members. Ask them to stand alongside the ladder at the level they determine the solution or strategy is, given the filters. Remind them that the bottom of the ladder is low impact and top of the ladder is high impact.

7. The facilitator notes or marks where most of staff are grouped (median in the range) and places a card or piece of paper with the strategy on the floor at that point in between the rungs of the ladder.

8. Continue until all of the items, solutions, or strategies are ranked. Switch out staff members for each one or keep the same group.

9. Create a graphic of the ladder and the ranked items, and send it out to staff for final discussion and consideration.

Alternative Methods for Ranking

- Use a vertical wall ladder made out of tape.
- Then give participants dots and have them place them alongside the ladder.
- With dots, you could use a different color for each category identified in Number 3.
- For a wall ladder, place an easily read piece of paper with the category labeled on a rung of the ladder where the most people stood or dots were placed.
- Follow Step 9 to follow up.
- For very large groups, break into small teams and create a ladder on paper, following Steps 2 through 5.

When

- You need to focus decisions that impact staff time, resources, and efforts with a common vision of excellence.
- This is good after lunch, at the end of the morning, or at the end of the day.
- Use anytime people need a change from the current condition and another colleague to consider multiple ideas and then create some sort of priority order.
- Multiple viewpoints would help problem solve or plan.
- There is a need for team building and common visioning.
- There is a need to revisit what excellence looks like in a building or on a team.
- The risk is high in choice making or prioritization, and using the median is a neutral approach.

Examples and Uses

1. Use to determine which work (reading, writing, math, student issues) takes precedence and which resources will be used in closing the achievement gap.

2. There are numerous competing issues around the growth of multiple subgroups in reading, writing, or math.

3. The district requires six goals, and equal energy and resources cannot be devoted to each without losing focus or momentum.

Selected References

Daniels (1986), Destra Consulting Group (2002), Texas Department of Education (2006).

THE PEOPLE LADDER

Step One: Develop solutions or strategies to address a goal or problem.

Step Two: What does excellence look like at this school (on this team) for students if we do a great job on our goal or solving our problem?

Step Three: Use these criteria for excellence to rank the strategies or solutions. This helps us prioritize and sequence work.

Example: Ideas for Improving Expository Writing

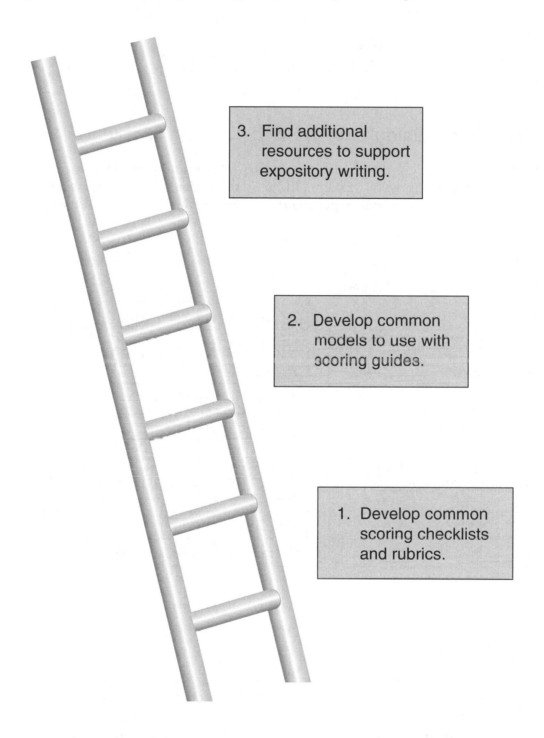

3. Find additional resources to support expository writing.

2. Develop common models to use with scoring guides.

1. Develop common scoring checklists and rubrics.

STRATEGY 60

Think Abouts

Purpose: Determining Priorities and Creating Excellence

This method helps individuals prepare for group problem solving or solution development. It increases the thinking level rapidly and helps participants sort through their thoughts prior to discussion. This improves the quality of the resulting solutions and proposals.

Basics

Number of Participants	Small groups and individuals
Time Needed	3–5 minutes
Room Arrangement	Small groups
Difficulty Level	Moderate level since it requires personal reflection and sharing about more complex issues
Brain Bits	Reflection, emotional and social contacts, and prioritizations are essential to learning
Adult Learning Principle	Choices, reflection, and prioritization make a difference in adult commitment to learning
Materials	Template
Other	Use for processing book studies or videos

Process Directions

1. Establish the purpose by explaining the need the group has for all participants to offer their perspectives and reflections to reach the target they have established or get the desired results.

2. Give participants one of the templates or sheets to fill out for the next session.

3. This helps the group ground and shifts into learning orientation more quickly.

4. Use for a short stretch, such as for three meetings in a row, and then evaluate the usefulness.

5. Always process the "Think About" to honor the time and perspective of participants. Use "Round Robin" to help move the conversation along.

When

- Use at regular intervals when you are finished with one step in a complex process and are about to start another step.
- A group has trouble sticking with the agenda.
- Issues are controversial and personal perspectives deserve some attention, but not so they dominate the limited amount of meeting time.
- You need to deepen thinking and understanding about the work.

Examples and Uses

1. Use to help a team process and prioritize ideas from a book study or video.
2. Use to reflect on student assessment results or student work samples.
3. Use to help prepare for decision making.
4. Use to facilitate the transfer of strategies and new learning to classrooms.

Selected References

Hill and Hill (1990), Hoffman and Olson-Ness (1996).

EXAMPLES OF THINK ABOUTS: PART 1

Directions

Put one of these at the top of a sheet of paper and give one to each member of the group to fill out before the next meeting or learning session.

EXAMPLE ONE

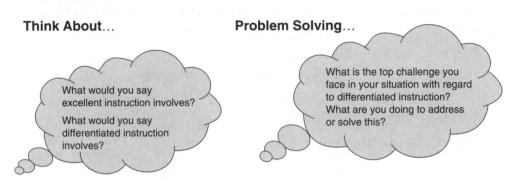

Think About…

What would you say excellent instruction involves?

What would you say differentiated instruction involves?

Problem Solving…

What is the top challenge you face in your situation with regard to differentiated instruction? What are you doing to address or solve this?

EXAMPLE TWO

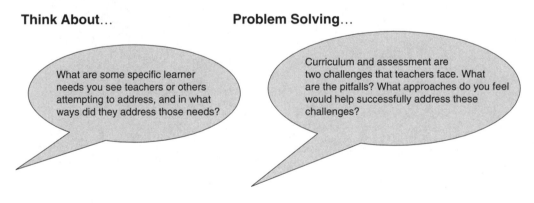

Think About…

What are some specific learner needs you see teachers or others attempting to address, and in what ways did they address those needs?

Problem Solving…

Curriculum and assessment are two challenges that teachers face. What are the pitfalls? What approaches do you feel would help successfully address these challenges?

EXAMPLE THREE

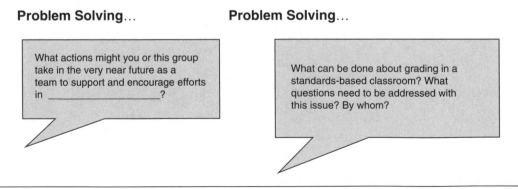

Problem Solving…

What actions might you or this group take in the very near future as a team to support and encourage efforts in _____?

Problem Solving…

What can be done about grading in a standards-based classroom? What questions need to be addressed with this issue? By whom?

EXAMPLES OF THINK ABOUTS: PART 2

Problem Solving Think Abouts

Use this chart prior to a meeting or at the start as a warm-up. Add any categories that match the major areas in problem solving or upcoming issues. The categories listed in the following are just examples.

Category	Challenges	Possible Suggestions
Curriculum		
Assessment		
Grouping of Students		
Discipline Issues		
Resources and Materials		
Grading		

STRATEGY 61

Data Chats

Purpose: Determining Priorities and Creating Excellence

"Data Chats" are an excellent way to use current data to make decisions and maintain focus. It is critical to success in student achievement to keep asking the right questions as the year goes on. These prompts will help teachers make the necessary course and strategy corrections throughout the year.

Basics

Number of Participants	Small groups or partners
Time Needed	30 minutes to one hour to set up, classroom observation time, debrief of one or more hours
Room Arrangement	Small groups
Difficulty Level	Average difficulty
Brain Bits	People need social relationships that validate and result in acceptance. We need to use "sense-making" actions to move forward in our learning. People need trustworthy environments in which to work and grow
Adult Learning Principle	Adults need to connect to what we do well, see the real needs for change and improvement
Materials	Current data from unit assessments, student work, or other ongoing data
Other	This strategy takes practice and may need to be modeled for effective replication

Process Directions

1. Review data from ongoing assessments throughout the year or review summative data to inform school planning and instructional focus.

2. Choose one or two of the questions to guide the discussion.

3. Discuss the next steps or actions the group will take as a result of the conclusions.

4. Review the success of any changes in instruction methods, materials, time, or peer coaching that the group chooses to implement.

When

- You need to determine if current strategies are working and students are making growth.
- You need to determine next steps in instruction or focus time and resources.
- You need to determine what sufficient growth is for each student.

Examples and Uses

1. Teachers review student work in writing to determine if the graphic organizers introduced to students helped to impact organizational skills.

2. Teachers review assessment data from reading tests to see if the phonics instruction is causing the amount of growth needed for students who are behind.

3. Teachers review student work or assessments from math to determine what review might be needed prior to the next unit.

Selected References

Columbia University, Teachers College Lesson Study Research Group (2005); Lewis (2002, 2003, 2005); Richardson (2000/2001, 2004).

QUESTIONS AND PROMPTS FOR DATA CHATS

Diagnostic Assessments and Student Work

1. What strategies seem to generate growth for special-education students in . . . (list content area)?

2. What evidence do you have that the gap is closing for English-Language Learners in reading or writing?

3. What next steps in instruction need to be taken, given the results of . . . (name the assessment)?

4. Given the growth for this group of students, which strategies did you use that caused this positive result? Will they work for all students or only students with certain learning needs?

5. How can we use these results to inform the amount of time we spend on given concepts and skills, the materials and resources we choose, and the strategies for teaching and learning we select?

QUESTIONS AND PROMPTS FOR DATA CHATS

Formal or Summative Assessments

1. **What does the test or assessment measure?**
   a. Does the test measure specific content or standards?
   b. Does the test measure broad concepts?
   c. Does the test measure problem solving?
   d. Are we teaching the things this test measures?

2. **How does the test assessment measure?**
   a. Is the test multiple choice or constructed response?
   b. Are students required to use reading or writing skills to demonstrate knowledge?
   c. What level of critical thinking does the test require?
   d. Is it knowledge, comprehension, application, synthesis, or evaluation?
   e. Does the test require single-step solutions or multistep solutions?
   f. Are we providing our students with opportunities to answer these types of questions or use this type of format throughout the school year?

3. **Why do we use this test—what kind of information do we gain?**
   a. Is the test a measure of growth or a measure of achievement?
   b. Does the test provide a measure of growth over time for individual students?
   c. Does the test measure cohort groups over time?
   d. Does the test provide grade-level comparisons from year to year?
   e. How will we use the information to plan our work or plan our instruction?

4. **Where are the grade-level expectations set—how good is good enough?**
   a. Are scores related to national norms? National percentiles?
   b. Can we see multiple-year trends?
   c. Are there correlations to other measures?
   d. Do we have student exemplars for various performance levels?

5. **What do the results tell us?**
   a. What are our students' strengths? Weaknesses?
   b. What other evidence do we have about these strengths or weaknesses?
   c. How does one group of students compare to other groups?
   d. Are the results consistent with other evidence? Logical? Expected? Surprising?
   e. What will we do with this information?

Putting It All Together

Supporting and sustaining change in an organization "requires a real sense of inquiry, a genuine curiosity about limiting forces. It requires seeing how significant change invariably starts locally, and how it grows over time. And it recognizes the diverse array of people who play key roles in sustaining change—people who are 'leaders.'"

—Peter Senge et al. (1999, p. 10)

Sustaining professional learning communities is at least as challenging as getting them started. This book is designed to give you targeted strategies that help any team work through the complexities of adult learning over the long haul. In this final chapter, we will describe the stages and phases many teams go through and how to apply some of the strategies and methods we have included.

There are three parts to planning and sustaining good professional learning:

1. Preassessment of needs and current stage of growth,

2. Carefully planned opportunities utilizing the right strategies for the desired results, and

3. Finally assessing the results and success of the adult learning in terms of students' progress.

Based on the information in the introduction to this book, we use adult learning principles to help us judge professional growth and the success of adult learning events.

- Was it useful and applicable to our situation?
- Were we given support and follow-up?
- Did we have time to exchange ideas and help each other with implementation and reflection?

Then, we use other resources to create a professional learning plan such as National Staff Development Council Standards, brain research, a wide variety of protocols and strategies, and natural learning systems. However, we need more information before we even start planning. We need to understand the learning styles of the adults we work with and the phases of group interaction. This preassessment will help us focus our planning and select strategies that meet the needs of the group, given what they are ready to accomplish and what they have achieved so far. This preassessment falls into one of two approaches, depending on whether groups are already established or are just forming.

PART 1: INITIAL GROUP DEVELOPMENT

As mentioned in the introduction, teams develop at different rates and require skillful facilitation. Once we determine the phase a newly formed or existing group is at, we can select the strategies that help us move the group forward to the next stage. At each stage of the wheel, there are things the team members and leaders can do to help the evolution process in a positive way with less frustration and less time lost.

Phases of Group Development and Behaviors

Developmental Phase	Strategies to Use
Establishing: Forming	Building Climate and Sharing Knowledge
Dissatisfaction: Storming	Building Climate, Problem Solving, Determining Priorities
Stabilizing: Norming	Determining Priorities, Creating Excellence, and Building Resilience
Production: Performing	Sharing Knowledge and Skills, Creating Excellence, and Sustaining Change

PART 2: SUSTAINING GROUPS OVER TIME AND THROUGH NEW INITIATIVES

As groups evolve past this initial formation, they go through other phases, and this can also be a time to carefully select the right strategies depending on the purpose and challenges the professional learning community is ready to tackle. These phases are often repeated as the group encounters new challenges, learning, and opportunities.

Phases of Learning for Existing Professional Learning Communities

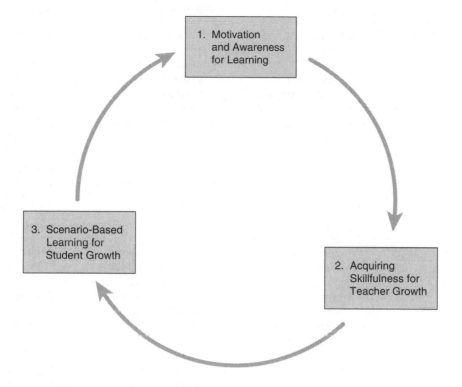

As teams encounter new topics and learning, established groups regularly cycle through three phases. This helps us determine the work they are ready to do, based on the anticipated results the group is seeking. When tackling something new, the first phase an existing group goes through is "Motivation and Awareness for Learning." The Motivation and Awareness Phase is characterized by activating need, enabling the creativity a group needs to tackle change, expanding knowledge, and encountering cognitive dissonance that is a normal initial part of new learning. The second phase is "Acquiring Skillfulness for Teacher Growth." This is characterized by needing support during beginning skill acquisition, building the group capability for supporting the implementation of learning in the classroom, and enculturating valued skills when the team gets results with students. The third phase is "Scenario-Based Learning for Student Growth." Great groups get to this stage, and it helps them problem solve around newly learned skills, integrate these skills with other initiatives, and innovate enough to produce adequate or accelerated student growth. Here is a chart that summarizes these phases that established groups cycle through when they are learning new skills and strategies.

Choose Training, Dialogue, and Learning Strategies to Match Your Purpose for Adult Learning

Phase	Purposes	Characteristics	Methods/Strategies
Motivation and Awareness for Learning	• Activating the need • Enabling change • Expanding knowledge • Building awareness • Understanding and using summative data • Creating cognitive dissonance	• Strategies are engaging • Strategies are frequently multimedia or take place in a special location • Strategies are low risk • Strategies help the group share best practices • Strategies encourage "what if" thinking.	• Charismatic keynote • Book study • Article processing • Data awareness • Research • Conference • Video or multimedia clip • Use strategies from Sharing Knowledge and Skills and revisit strategies from Creating a Growth-Oriented Climate as needed.
Acquiring Skillfulness for Teacher Growth	• Beginning skill acquisition • Building group or learning community capacity • Understanding and using student work and lesson studies as data sources • Enculturating valued skills	• Protocols have a step-by-step process • Protocols have established "how to and why" questions • Protocols use the materials and examples from the learners' world • Strategies help the group process and reflect on student work and lesson success • Strategies can be medium to high risk depending on the trust level of the learning community	• Student work analysis • Lesson analysis • Cognitive coaching • Data analysis • Effective instruction practices • Inquiry and problem-based learning • Case studies • Critical friends evaluation • Use strategies from Building Resilience and Creating Solutions and revisit strategies from Creating a Growth-Oriented Climate as needed
Scenario-Based Learning for Student Growth	• Getting unstuck • Establishing high-performance teams • Integrating multiple initiatives • Understanding and using diagnostic assessment and incremental student growth as data sources • Innovating and creating excellence	• Focuses on desired future • Causes rapid shift in practice or beliefs • First steps use examples outside of the learners' world • Helps manage higher risk • Strategies help the group reflect on the adequacy and acceleration of student growth as a measure of successful classroom practices • The group and individuals ask "Why not?," "What else?," "Is this good enough?," and "How could we?" questions	• Asking open-ended questions using metaphors, fables, analogies, myths, case studies, and stories • Journey mapping • Charting the future • Determining impacts and results • Successful planning based on diagnostic results • Innovation methods • Use strategies from Determining Priorities and Creating Excellence and revisit strategies from Creating a Growth-Oriented Climate as needed

Using the *Learning Teams That Get Results* pyramid figure in the introduction chapter of this book, the strategies in the four previous chapters are the base of the pyramid and help us determine "What It Takes." At the initial stages of forming a group of adult learners, we can then use Turnball's model to help guide our preassessment. The results of this assessment help us form the learning teams that communicate and operate effectively. This corresponds to the "What It Looks Like" portion of the pyramid. As groups are formed and are ongoing, we use the "Learning Strategies to Match Adult Learning" chart to help us preassess and guide our next steps that learning teams go through. This corresponds to the "What We Want" and "What We Get" portions of the pyramid. The results of this assessment can then guide the selection of strategies as we plan to move teacher effectiveness forward and thereby increase student growth and achievement.

Learning Teams That Get Results

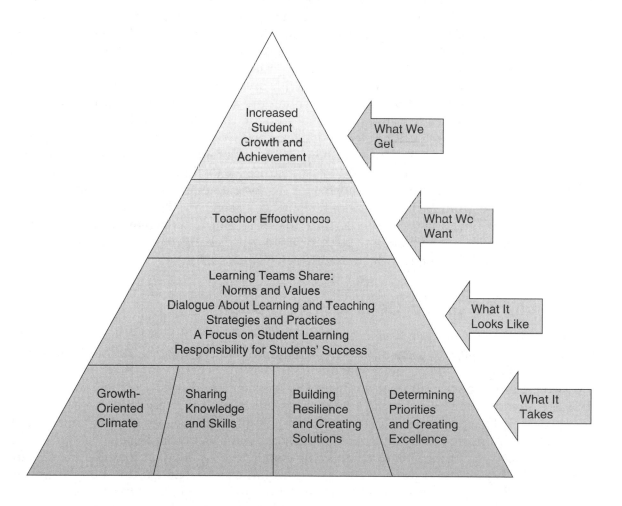

Showers and Joyce (1996) discuss the need for professional learning teams to combine action and analysis. Concentrating only on action allows no time for a group to check its progress or impact. If groups engage solely in analysis, they will never come to recognize their individual and collective power to create change and develop the results they seek for students. Groups that sustain themselves over time combine action and analysis or reflection. The right questions at the right phase of learning sustain change and include the enculturation of success. The phases described include strategies and methods that support these dual indicators of successful groups that sustain the momentum for learning over time.

PUTTING IT ALL TOGETHER: EXAMPLES FOR IMPLEMENTATION

A New Group Forming for a Specific Purpose

A high school group has been formed to determine changes that need to be made to the ninth-grade year. Too many students are dropping out and failing courses in ninth grade. The team is formed from a variety of departments, administration, district, and other personnel. This team needs to develop and go through the Turnball phases. Use strategies such as "T Chart and Y Chart" and "Find Someone Who" to get the teaming started. Also try a "Four-Corner Cards" to reflect on knowledge the group may already have. The "Pluses and Wishes" strategy may get the group started with awareness of the tough issues. As the group makes it through the storming and norming process, are they still using summative data? Once the group is ready to use individual student examples of work and teacher practice reflection, you can use such strategies as "Pros and Cons" or "Two Sides of the Story." If the group is ready to use student interview (a form of scenario-based learning), then try "Probable and Preferred Future" or a "Cause-and-Effect Planning" method of reflection. The group may also want to establish norms for working together as well by using nominal group process. The group will need enough resilience to confront the causes of the underlying problem before creating the solution. Once that is accomplished, creating excellence will be possible, but solutions will need to be prioritized, since changes in ninth-grade practices take a few years to implement well enough to see results.

An Established Group Getting More Skillful

The grade-level teams at a K–8 school have been working together for a couple of years. They are learning and implementing new comprehension strategies for nonfiction text. Several workshops are being held over the course of the school year. After each session, groups try to incorporate strategies into their classrooms and reflect on the success. The teams are already supportive of each other and want to acquire these skills. In addition to using protocols for reviewing student work and possibly using lesson studies, these teams may benefit from using strategies that build resilience and sustain change since this is hard work. They need to get the skill to an enculturation level as quickly as possible for student results. At the beginning of the year, the groups could use the "Consulting Line," "Graffiti Board," and "Pros and Cons" to help them reflect on their progress. As they move through the year and get ready to determine which strategies have the highest growth payoff for which students, such reflection methods as "Celebrations and Next Steps" and "Building on Success" may help them get ready to reinforce this learning next year, focusing on student growth.

An Ongoing Team That Needs to Close the Learning Gap for Diverse Students

A department team is frustrated because students are not growing as rapidly as needed to close achievement gaps. The team members revisit causes but sometimes get hung up, focusing on issues over which they have no control, such as the poverty-ridden lives of many of their students. The team may need to revisit some growth-oriented climate strategies to help them move back to what they can control and focus on, such as "Nominal Group Process," "Community Circle," or "Random Partners." If they can re-norm the team, then strategies such as "Concept Formation," "Parking Lot," "Current Snapshot," "SWOT," and "Prioritizing the Impact of Solutions" would work well. These methods will help the department team get unstuck, create priorities, and then move forward with effective solutions.

Teams Shifting From Teacher Effectiveness to Student Results

Established teams that have effectively reviewed student work and lessons are ready to move forward to discuss what "enough" student growth looks like and how to get there. Effective strategies might focus on determining priorities and creating excellence and may include "the Interview," "Prioritizing the Impact of Solutions," and "Building on Success." To sustain the change, the team may need to also utilize "Promissory Note" or "Concept Formation."

New Teams Trying to Create a Focus on Literacy

Secondary teams at a high school or middle school may be formed to create a greater focus on literacy, including thinking and communication, since students need to achieve at higher levels in all content areas and on various high-stakes assessments. Getting secondary groups to have sufficient buy-in to literacy is essential. Secondary team formation to focus on literacy may require the use of such strategies as "A-B-C Conversations," "Round Robin," and "Wallpaper Poster," since these strategies help groups share knowledge and skills that exist. "Roadblock Removal" may also help overcome resistance, and "Success Planning" would build on techniques that were well proven at the school.

Rationale for Careful Strategy Selection

So, knowing whether a group has properly formed and what phase of learning they may be in helps us select strategies that match the needs of the group and support the desired results. Choosing to complete "Cause-and-Effect Planning" without establishing positive communication could increase roadblocks to learning rather than promote positive solutions. Taking time to do both has higher payoff and gets better results over longer periods of time.

KEEPING NOTES, LOGGING, AND OUR METHODS

Tracking the work of each learning team is important. This should be a simple and easy way to complete process. This way, teams can review these documents to track progress, celebrate success, and replicate successful practices by the professional learning team or community. The following are some examples of easy templates to track the work of the team. Other protocols for reviewing student work and lesson studies are available online through the National Staff Development Council and Critical Friends Organization, just to name a couple of sources.

EXAMPLE 1

Interaction Guidelines for Learning Teams

Guidelines	Learning Team Plan
Goals Write a critical question we will answer.	
Review What has already occurred and what was accomplished?	
Results What will it look like if we successfully answer the critical question?	
Actions Brainstorm possible actions.	
Reflection List pros and cons of actions and select or prioritize actions to work on.	
Next Steps Decide what will happen between this meeting and the next.	

Other Notes and Reminders for Learning Team Members:

EXAMPLE 2

Evaluating Student Work

Insights and Reflections:

Challenges and Worries:

Solutions and Next Steps:

EXAMPLE 3

Transfer to My Classroom

Best Idea From My Team	How I Will Use This in My Classroom
1.	
2.	
3.	

KEEPING YOUR SCHOOL AND TEAM CULTURE AND CLIMATE HEALTHY

Keeping a pulse on the climate and culture of a building is essential. Here is tool that may help monitor the health of groups or the school as a whole. Use it to help select strategies that prompt adult growth as well as student growth. "In school cultures valuing collegiality and collaboration, there is a better climate for the social and professional exchange of ideas, the enhancement and spread of effective practices, and widespread professional problem solving" (Deal & Peterson, 1998, p. 7).

Assessing School and Team Culture and Climate

Rate each of the following attributes of a healthy school or team climate using the following system:

4 = You could teach others things.   3 = You are consistently seeing these.
2 = You occasionally experience this.   1 = You are just getting started.

❑ Staff reflect on the quality of professional dialogue.

❑ Staff celebrate incremental successes with students.

❑ Staff celebrate incremental successes with peers.

❑ Staff pass the culture and history of the school to new staff.

❑ Staff seek to contribute and collaborate.

❑ Staff offer assistance to each other and ask for assistance.

❑ Use of norms or informal agreements help keep communication positive and professional.

❑ Appropriate uses of humor and team activities are supportive.

❑ Administrators monitor the climate and culture and seek to make needed changes or time for dialogue.

❑ Administrators provide frequent and appropriate feedback.

❑ The majority of staff questions are about aspects of complex thinking and problem solving rather than procedure.

❑ Staff collaborate as needed without prompts.

❑ Staff attitudes and demeanor are generally positive based on comments by parents and other outside personnel.

❑ Staff exhibit purposeful action toward professional and school goals.

SUMMARY

In conclusion, we advocate group learning and individual competence as the cornerstone of adult learning. An effective approach to building and sustaining teams that focus on student results and teacher excellence helps promote an atmosphere of inquiry and rigor throughout the school. Wald and Castleberry (2000, p. 136) write:

> Inquiring classrooms are not likely to flourish in schools where inquiry among teachers and stakeholders is discouraged. A commitment to problem solving is difficult to instill in students who are taught by teachers for whom problem solving is not allowed. Where there is little discourse among teachers, discourse among students will be harder to promote and maintain. . . . The idea of making classrooms into learning communities for students will remain more rhetoric than real unless schools become learning communities for teachers too.

Daryl Conner (1998) writes about three kinds of groups and their growing sophistication in handling issues and creating growth. He says that working groups give ad hoc support to sites, departments, and individuals. Expert groups provide what working groups do and provide expertise as needed to each other, sharing and learning to support each other. Finally, Conner discusses high-performance teams that combine the efforts of the first two groups and become a team by knowing how to prioritize, allocating resources and demonstrating superiority at making course-changing decisions and implementing creative solutions. We hope that your groups become high-performance teams that get amazing results.

Take time to celebrate your successes. Building off your success, determining what actions caused success, and then replicating the appropriate actions again to tackle the next problem are forms of asset mapping. Successful schools know how they became successful and seek to replicate those actions. Knowing what contributes to successful practices is critical. Here are some examples of celebrations high-performing schools use to judge successful team practices.

Educators are heroic in their efforts to integrate emotion, relationship, and human interaction to influence learning. Brown and Moffat (1999) wrote, "If our attempts to go wider in our change efforts are to be educationally productive. . . . we must also go deeper and examine the moral grounds and emotional texture of our practice, of what it means to be a teacher." We thank you for your "heroic" efforts and hope that as you deepen your thinking, working with other heroes, you get the results you seek for our children and for their future.

We believe that the process of increasing student growth and achievement is directly proportional to the amount of effort and time spent on teacher effectiveness. That involves giving high-quality time and meaningful practices for teachers to perfect their craft and become a true professional learning community. We hope these tools help you become a learning team that gets results. We salute your efforts and your desire to increase growth and achievement for students!

Adjusting Celebrations in High Achieving Schools

Focusing Elements for Praise and Celebration	What to Celebrate?
Fostering Problem Solving	• Metacognition about problem solving and solution development • Questioning the assumptions of yourself and others • Discovering errors and understanding what aspects contribute to the error • Discussing pros and cons of solutions • Supporting and respecting diverse ideas
Extending Elaboration and Generalization	• Testing ideas • Finding evidence to support a point of view • Developing a criteria for evaluation • Using prior learning to inform or form a new situation • Building on other ideas and the ideas of others • Posing higher level questions—monitor verbs in questions
Supporting Creativity	• Generating ideas • Shifting perspective easily and using data to adjust thinking • Conceiving something new or using something in a unique way • Being flexible in solution creation and implementation • Persevering even as difficulty levels rise
Developing Schema	• Describing what you used and why to come up with an answer, solution, process, etc. • Trying a strategy and acknowledging if it does not get the desired results, and then trying another strategy or seeking out a new method • Using multiple strategies and solutions • Enculturating what works and teaching it to new staff • Using appropriate strategies given change, challenge, or success

SOURCE: Adapted from Gregory & Kuzmich (2004).

References

Alberta Department of Education in Canada. (2002). *An example of an environmental scan.* Retrieved April 2006 from http://www.education.ualberta.co/educ/reserach/tri-fac/enviro.html

Albright, R., & Shaller, R. (1998, October 30). *Technology roadmap workshop.* Arlington, VA: Office of Naval Research.

Ambrose, D. (2002). *Cross impact matrix.* Paper presented at the Center for Innovative Instruction, Rider University, Princeton, NJ.

Annenberg Institute for School Reform. (1998). *Critical friends groups in action: Facilitator's guide.* Providence, RI: Brown University.

Arbuckle, M., & Murray, L. (1989). *Building systems for professional growth: An action guide.* Andover, MA: Regional Laboratory for Educational Improvement of the Northeast & Islands.

Aronson, E., Blaney, N., Stephin, C., Sikes, J., & Snapp, M. (1978). *The jigsaw classroom.* Beverly Hills, CA: Sage.

Australian Government Department of Education. (2006). *My read.* Retrieved August 28, 2006, from http://www.myread.org/index.htm

Bailey, S. (1990, December). *Beyond training: Professional developers as gardeners, storytellers and cultural architects.* Paper presented at the National Staff Development Council Conference in Toronto, Canada.

Bailey, S. (1995). *Forging unified commitment from diverse perspectives: New approaches to helping groups through change* (ASCD Satellite Broadcast Series). Alexandria, VA: ASCD.

Barell, J. (2003). *Developing more curious minds.* Alexandria, VA: ASCD.

Barker, J. (1992). *Future edge: Discovering the new paradigms of success.* New York: Morrow Books.

Barth, R. (2001). *Learning by heart.* San Francisco, CA: Jossey-Bass.

Barth, R. (2003). *Lessons learned.* Thousand Oaks, CA: Corwin Press.

Beaudoin, M., & Taylor, M. (2004). *Creating a positive school culture: How principals and teachers can solve problems together.* Thousand Oaks, CA: Corwin Press.

Bellanca, J. (1990). *The cooperative think tank.* Thousand Oaks, CA: Corwin Press.

Bellanca, J., & Fogarty, R. (1994). *Blueprints for thinking in the cooperative classroom.* Heatherton, Australia: Hawker Brownlow Education.

Bennett, B., Joyce, B., & Showers, B. (2002). *Student achievement through staff development.* Alexandria, VA: ASCD.

Bennett, B., & Rolheiser, C. (2001). *Beyond Monet.* Toronto, Canada: Bookation.

Bennett, B., Rolheiser, C., & Stevahn, L. (1991). *Cooperative learning: Where heart meets mind.* Toronto, Canada: Educational Connections.

Bidart, P. (2003). *Assignment II.* Retrieved August 26, 2002, from http://www.unr.edu/cll/ci602/ci602 projectspdfandword/story%20star%20graphic%20organizer.doc

Blake, R., Mouton, J., & Allen, R. (1987). *Spectacular teamwork: How to develop the leadership skills for team success.* New York: John Wiley & Sons.

Bloom, B. S. (1984). *Taxonomy of educational objectives.* Boston: Allyn and Bacon.

Bridges, W. (1991). *Managing transitions: Making the most of change.* Boston: Addison-Wesley.

Bridges, W., & Mitchell, S. (2000, Spring). Leading transition: A new model for change. *Leader to Leader, 16,* 30–36.

Brookfield, S. (1988). Understanding and facilitating adult learning. *School Library Media Quarterly,* *16*(2), 99–105.

Brown, J., & Moffat, C. (1999). *The hero's journey: How educators can transform schools and improve learning.* Alexandria, VA: ASCD.

Bryk, A. S., & Schneider, B. L. (2002). *Trust in schools: A core resource for improvement.* New York: Russell Sage Foundation.

Buehl, D. (2006). *Hearing "voices" as you read.* Retrieved August 28, 2006, from http://wilearns.state .wi.us/apps/default.asp?cid=718

Burke, K. (1993). *The mindful school: How to assess thoughtful outcomes.* Palatine, IL: IRI/Skylight.

Buzan, T. (1991). *Use both sides of your brain* (3rd ed.). New York: Penguin Books.

Chadwick, B. (2006). *"The circle" and "grounding."* Retrieved April 2006 from http://www.managing wholes.com/power.htm

Chang, R., & Buster, S. (1999). *Step-by-step problem solving in education.* Houston, TX: APQC.

Chang, R., & Dalziel, D. (1999a). *Continuous improvement tools in education, Vol. 1.* Houston, TX: APQC.

Chang, R., & Dalziel, D. (1999b). *Continuous improvement tools in education, Vol. 2.* Houston, TX: APQC.

Chapman, A. (2005). *SWOT analysis method.* Retrieved April 2006 from http://www.businessballs.com

Colan, L. (2003). *Sticking to it: The art of adherence.* Dallas, TX: CornerStone Leadership Institute.

Cole, R. E. (2002). *Strategies for learning: Small-group activities in American, Japanese, and Swedish industry.* Berkeley: University of California Press.

Columbia University, Teachers College Lesson Study Research Group. (2005). *Lesson study groups.* Retrieved August 28, 2006, from http://www.tc.edu/lessonstudy/lsgroups.html

Conner, D. (1993). *Managing at the speed of change.* New York: Villard Books.

Conner, D. (1998). *Leading at the edge of chaos: How to create the nimble organization.* New York: John Wiley & Sons.

Costa, A., & Garmston, R. (2002). *Cognitive coaching: A foundation for renaissance schools* (2nd ed.). Norwood, MA: Christopher-Gordon.

Covey, S. (1989). *The seven habits of highly effective people: Restoring the character ethic.* New York: Simon and Schuster.

Csikszentmihalyi, M. (1991). *Flow: The psychology of optimal experience.* New York: HarperCollins.

Dalellew, R., & Martinez, Y. (1998). Andragogy and development: A search for the meaning of staff development. *Journal of Staff Development, 9*(3), 28–31.

Damasio, A. (1999). *The feeling of what happens: Body and emotion in the making of consciousness.* New York: Harcourt Brace.

Daniels, W. (1986). *Group power I: A manager's guide to using task force meetings.* San Diego, CA: University Associates, Inc., and Johnson & Johnson.

Deal, T., & Peterson, K. (1998). *Shaping school culture: The heart of leadership.* San Francisco: Jossey-Bass.

Deal, T., & Peterson, K. (2002). *The shaping school culture fieldbook.* San Francisco, CA: Jossey-Bass.

De Bono, E. (1987). *CoRT thinking program.* Boston: Little, Brown.

Destra Consulting Group. (2002, April). *Presentation on "dealing with rapid change."* Thompson School District, Loveland, CO.

Dosher, M., Benepe, O., Humphrey, A., Stewart, R., & Lie, B. (1960–1970). *The SWOT analysis method.* Menlo Park, CA: Stanford Research Institute.

DuFour, R., Eaker, R. E., & Baker, R. (1998). *Professional learning communities at work: Best practices for enhancing student achievement.* Bloomington, IN: National Educational Service.

Dunne, F., Nave, B., & Lewis, A. (2000, December). Critical friends groups: Teachers helping teachers to improve student learning. *Research Bulletin, 28,* 4.

Elder, L., & Paul, R. (2002). *Instructor's manual for critical thinking tools for taking charge of your learning and your life.* San Francisco: Foundation for Critical Thinking.

English, R., & Dean, S. (2004). *Show me how to learn: Key strategies and powerful techniques that promote cooperative learning.* Portland, ME: Stenhouse.

Enchanted Learning. (2006a). *T-chart.* Retrieved August 28, 2006, from http://www.enchanted learning.com/graphicorganizers/tchart/

Enchanted Learning. (2006b). *Y-chart.* Retrieved August 28, 2006, from http://www.enchanted learning.com/graphicorganizers/ychart/

Erickson, L. (2005). *Concept based curriculum and instruction.* Thousand Oaks, CA: Corwin Press.

Fullan, M. (1993). Innovation, reform, and restructuring strategies. In G. Cawelti (Ed.), *Challenges and achievements of American education.* Alexandria, VA: ASCD.

Fullan, M. (2002). *Student achievement through staff development.* Alexandria, VA: ASCD.

Garcia, M., & Bray, O. (1997). *Fundamentals of technology roadmapping.* Albuquerque, NM: Sandia National Laboratories.

Garmston, R. (1996). Triple track presenting. *Journal of Staff Development, 17*(2).

Garmston, R. (1997). *The presenter's fieldbook: A practical guide.* Norwood, MA: Christopher-Gordon.

Garmston, R., & Wellman, B. (1999). *The adaptive school: Developing and facilitating collaborative groups.* Norwood, MA: Christopher-Gordon.

Gibbs, J. (2001). *Tribes: A new way of learning and being together.* Windsor, CA: Center Source Systems, LLC.

Given, B. (2002). *The brain's natural learning systems.* Alexandria, VA: ASCD.

Goleman, D. (1995). *Emotional intelligence.* New York: Bantam.

Gordon, T., & Hayward, R. (1968, December). *Initial experiments with the cross-impact matrix method of forecasting.* Paper presented at the University of California, Los Angeles, CA.

Gordon, W. (1961). *Synectics.* New York: Harper and Row.

Graphic Organizer. (2006). *KWHL chart.* Retrieved August 28, 2006, from http://www.graphic.org/kwhl.html

Gregorc, A. (1982). *Inside styles: Beyond the basics.* Columbia, CT: Gregorc Associates.

Gregory, G. (2000, December). *Enhancing teacher quality.* Presentation at the National Staff Development Council annual conference.

Gregory, G. (2006). *Differentiating instruction with style.* Thousand Oaks, CA: Corwin Press.

Gregory, G., & Chapman, C. (2007). *Differentiated Instructional strategies: One size doesn't fit all, 2nd ed.* Thousand Oaks, CA: Corwin Press.

Gregory, G., & Kuzmich, L. (2004). *Data driven differentiation in the standards-based classroom.* Thousand Oaks, CA: Corwin Press.

Gregory, G., & Kuzmich, L. (2005a). *Differentiated literacy strategies for student achievement grades K–6.* Thousand Oaks, CA: Corwin Press.

Gregory, G., & Kuzmich, L. (2005b). *Differentiated literacy strategies for student achievement grades 7–12.* Thousand Oaks, CA: Corwin Press.

Gregory, G., & Parry, T. (2006). *Designing brain compatible learning.* Thousand Oaks, CA: Corwin Press.

Gregory, G., Robbins, P., & Herndon, L. (2000). *Teaching inside the block schedule: Strategies for teaching in extended periods of time.* Thousand Oaks, CA: Corwin Press.

Guild, P., & Garger, S. (1985). *Marching to different drummers.* Alexandria, VA: ASCD.

Hargreaves, A. (1997). Rethinking educational change. In A. Hargreaves (Ed.), *Rethinking educational change with heart and mind: 1997 ASCD yearbook* (pp. 14–33). Alexandria, VA: ASCD.

Hargreaves, A., & Dawe, R. (1989). Paths of professional development: Contrived collegiality, collaborative culture, and the case of peer coaching. *Teaching and Teacher Education, 6,* 227–241.

Harris, J. (1998). *The nature assumption: Why children turn out the way they do.* New York: Free Press.

Hartzler, M., & Henry, J. (1994). *Team fitness: A how-to manual for building a winning work team.* Milwaukee, WI: ASQC Quality Press.

Hertz-Lazarowitz, R., Kagan, S., Sharan, S., Slavin, R., & Webb, C. (Eds.). (1985). *Learning to cooperate: Cooperating to learn.* New York: Plenum.

Hill, S., & Eckert, P. (1995). *Leading communities of learners.* Adelaide, Australia: Management and Research Centre.

Hill, S. & Hancock, J. (1993). *Reading and writing communities.* Armadale, Australia.

Hill, S., & Hill, T. (1990). *The collaborative classroom: A guide to cooperative learning.* Portsmouth, NH: Heinemann.

Hoffman, C., & Olson-Ness, J. (1996). *Tips and tools for trainers and teams.* Tacoma, WA: VISTA Associates.

Hord, S., Rutherford, W., Huling-Austin, L., & Hall, G. (1987). *Taking charge of change.* Alexandria, VA: ASCD.

James, J. (1996). *Thinking in the future tense: A workout for the mind.* New York: Touchstone Books, Simon and Schuster.

Johns, J., VanLeirsburg, P., & Davis, S. (1994). *Improving reading: A handbook of strategies.* Dubuque, IA: Kendall/Hunt.

Johnson, D., & Johnson, R. (1991). *Cooperative learning.* Edina, MN: Interaction Book Company.

Johnson, D., & Johnson, R. (1994). *Leading the cooperative school.* Edina, MN: Interaction Book Company.

Johnson, D., Johnson, R., & Johnson-Holubec, E. (1993). *Circles of learning: Cooperation in the classroom.* Edina, MN: Interaction Book Company.

Johnson, D., Johnson, R., & Smith, K. (1991a). *Active learning: Cooperation in the college classroom.* Edina, MN: Interaction Book Company.

Johnson, D., Johnson, R., & Smith, K. (1991b). *Cooperative learning: Increasing college faculty instructional productivity.* Edina, MN: Interaction Book Company.

Jones, R. (1998). *3-2-1.* Retrieved August 28, 2006, from http://curry.edschool.virginia.edu/go/read quest/strat/321.html

Jones, R. (2005). *Planning with rigor and relevance.* Albany, NY: International Center for Leadership in Education.

Junior Reserve Officers Training Corps. (2006). *Lesson 5: Graphic organizers.* Retrieved August 28, 2006, from http://www.rotc.monroe.army.mil/JROTC/documents/Curriculum/Unit_3/u3c5l5.pdf

Kagan, S. (1992). *Cooperative learning.* San Clemente, CA: Kagan Cooperative.

Kanter, R. (1984). *Change masters.* New York: Simon and Schuster.

Kassouf, S. (1970). *Normative decision making.* Englewood Cliffs, NJ: Prentice-Hall.

Killion, J. (2002). *Assessing impact: Evaluating staff development.* Oxford, OH: National Staff Development Council.

Knowles, M. (1980). Life long learning. *Training and Development Journal, 34*(7), 40.

Kolb, D. (1984). *Experiential learning: Experience as the source of learning and development.* EnglewoodCliffs, NJ: Prentice Hall.

Kuzmich, L. (1999). *School improvement planning using results.* Longmont, CO: CBOCES.

Kuzmich, L. (2003). *Scenario based learning.* Paper presented at Fall Conference for New Orleans Archdiocese, New Orleans, LA.

Langer, G., Colton, A., & Goff, L. (2003). *Collaborative analysis of student work: Improving teaching and learning.* Alexandria, VA: ASCD.

Lewis, C. (2002, Summer). Everywhere I looked—levers and pendulums. *Journal of Staff Development,* 59–65.

Lewis, C. (2003). *The essential elements of lesson study.* Retrieved December 30, 2005, from the Northwest Regional Education Laboratory Web site: http://www.nwrel.org/msec/nwteacher/spring2003/elements.html

Lewis, C. (2005). *Lesson study: Crafting learning together.* Retrieved August 28, 2006, from the Northwest Regional Education Laboratory Web site: http://www.nwrel.org/msec/nwteacher/spring2003/elements.html

Lipton, L., Humbard, C., & Wellman, B. (2001). *Mentoring matters: A practical guide to learning-focused relationships.* Sherman, CT: MiraVia, LLC.

Lowry, D. (1979). *The keys to personal success.* Riverside, CA: True Colors.

Lyman, F. (1981). The responsive classroom discussion: The inclusion of all students. In A. Anderson (Ed.), *Mainstreaming digest* (pp. 109–113). College Park: University of Maryland Press.

Lyman, F., & McTighe, J. (2001). Cueing thinking in the classroom: The promise of theory-embedded tools. In A. L. Costa (Ed.), *Developing minds: A resources book for teaching thinking* (3rd ed., Chapter 61). Alexandria, VA: ASCD.

Marzano, R. (2004). *Building background knowledge for academic achievement.* Alexandria, VA: ASCD.

Marzano, R. J., Norford, J. S., Paynter, D. E., Gaddy, B. B., & Pickering, D. J. (Eds.) (2004). *A handbook for classroom instruction that works.* Alexandria, VA: ASCD.

McCarthy, B. (2000). *About teaching: 4MAT in the classroom.* Wanconda, FL: About Learning.

Mind Tools. (2006a). *Force field analysis: Understanding the pressures for and against change.* Retrieved August 28, 2006, from http://www.mindtools.com/forcefld.html

Mind Tools. (2006b). *Personal goal setting.* Retrieved August 28, 2006, from http://www.mindtools.com/page6.html

Mind Tools. (2006c). *PMI: Weighing the pros and cons of a decision.* Retrieved August 28, 2006, from http://www.mindtools.com/pmi.html

Murphy, C. (2005). *Connecting teacher leadership and school improvement.* Alexandria, VA: ASCD.

Murphy, C., & Lick, D. (1998). *Whole faculty study groups: A powerful way to change schools and enhance student learning.* Thousand Oaks, CA: Corwin Press.

Murphy, N. (1994). *Authentic assessment for the learning cycle model.* Columbus, OH: ERIC Clearinghouse for Science, Mathematics, and Environmental Education.

National School Board Association. (2005). *Taking stock: Environmental scans.* Retrieved April 2006 from http://www.nsba.org/sbot/toolkit/ts.html

National School Reform Faculty: Harmony Center. (2005). *Program on creating critical friends groups.* Retrieved December 30, 2005, from http://www.nsrfharmony.org/faq.html#1

NCREL. (2006). *KWL.* Retrieved August 28, 2006, from http://www.ncrel.org/sdrs/areas/issues/students/learning/lr2kwl.htm

Newmann, F., & Wehlage, G. (1995). *Successful school restructuring.* Alexandria, VA: ASCD.

Ogle, D. (1986). K-W-L: A teaching model that develops active reading of expository text. *The Reading Teacher, 39,* 564–570.

Osborn, A. F. (1963). *Applied imagination: Principles and procedures of creative problem solving* (3rd ed.). New York: Scribner.

Panksepp, J. (1998). *Affective neuroscience: The foundations of human and animal emotions.* New York: Oxford University Press.

Perkins, D. (1995). *Outsmarting IQ.* New York: Freedom Press.

Pert, C. (1993). The chemical communicators. In B. Moyers (Ed.), *Healing and the mind* (pp. 158–162). New York: Doubleday.

Peterson, K., & Deal, T. (2002). *The shaping school culture fieldbook.* San Francisco, CA: Jossey-Bass.

Pink, D. (2005). *A whole new mind: Moving from the Information Age to the Conceptual Age.* New York: Riverhead Books.

Reeves, D. (2002). *The daily disciplines of leadership: How to improve student achievement, staff motivation, and personal organization.* San Francisco, CA: Jossey-Bass.

Reid, J. (2002). *Managing small group learning.* Newtown, Australia: Primary English Teaching Association.

Renzulli, J. S. (1994). *Schools for talent development: A practical plan for total school improvement.* Mansfield Center, CT: Creative Learning Press.

Richardson, J. (2000/2001). *Lesson study: Japanese method has benefit for all students.* Oxford, OH: National Staff Development Council.

Richardson, J. (2004, February/March). *Lesson study: Tools for schools.* Oxford, OH: National Staff Development Council.

Robbins, P. (1991). *How to plan and implement a peer coaching program.* Alexandria, VA: ASCD.

Roberts, S., & Pruitt, E. (2003). *Schools as professional learning communities, collaborative activities and strategies for professional development.* Thousand Oaks, CA: Corwin Press.

Robertson, L., & Kagan, S. (1992). *Cooperative learning.* San Clemente, CA: Kagan Cooperative.

Roukes, N. (1988). *Design synectics: Stimulating creativity in design.* Worchester, MA: Davis Puhns.

Rowe, M. B. (1987). Wait time: Slowing down may be a way of speeding up. *American Educator, 11,* 38–73, 47.

Senge, P., Kleiner, A., Roberts, C., Ross, R., Roth, G., & Smith, B. (1999). *A fifth discipline resource: The dance of change—The challenges to sustaining momentum in learning organizations.* New York: Doubleday/Currency.

Shields, P., Esch, C., Humphrey, D., Young, V., Gaston, M., & Hunt, H. (1999). *The status of the teaching profession: Research findings and policy recommendations: A report to the Teaching and California's Future Task Force.* Santa Cruz, CA: Center for the Future of Teaching and Learning.

Showers, B., & Joyce, B. (1996). The evolution of peer coaching. *Educational Leadership, 53*(6), 12–16.

Showers, B., & Joyce, B. (2003). *Student achievement through staff development* (3rd ed.) Alexandria, VA: ASCD.

Silver, H., Strong, R., & Perini, M. (1997). *Cooperative learning.* Ho-Ho-Kus, NJ: Thoughtful Education Press.

Silver, H. F., & Hanson, J. R. (1998). *Learning styles and strategies* (3rd ed.). Woodbridge, NJ: The Thoughtful Education Press.

Slavin, R. (1994). *A practical guide to cooperative learning.* Boston, MA: Allyn and Bacon.

Sousa, D. (2004). *Brain research.* Paper presented at the National Staff Development Council preconference session, New Orleans, LA.

Sparks, D. (1998, Fall). Interview with Bruce Joyce: Making assessment part of teacher learning. *Journal of Staff Development, 19*(4), 33–35.

Taba, H. (1967). *Teacher's handbook for elementary social studies.* Reading, MA: Addison-Wesley.

Texas Department of Education. (2006). *The teaching-learning system: Curriculum, instruction and assessment.* Retrieved April 2006 from http://www.tea.state.tx.us/ssc/downloads/pdf/framework/Chapter5.pdf#xml

Tomlinson, C. (2001). *How to differentiate in mixed ability classrooms.* (2nd ed.). Alexandria, VA: ASCD.

Torrance, E. P. (1998). *Why fly? A philosophy of creativity.* Norwood, NJ: Ablex.

Tuckman, B.W. (1965). Developmental sequence in small groups. *Psychological Bulletin, 63,* 384–399.

Van de Ven, A. H., & Delbecq, A. L. (1974). The effectiveness of nominal, delphi and interacting group decision-making processes. *Academy of Management Journal, 17,* 4, 605–621.

Wald, M., & Castleberry, P. (2000). *Educators as learners: Creating a professional learning community in your school.* Alexandria, VA: ASCD.

Wellman, B., & Lipton, L. (2003, December). *Using data, processing methods.* Paper presented at the National Staff Development Council annual conference, New Orleans, LA.

Witmer, J., Rich, C., Barcikowski, R., & Mague, J. (1983). Psychosocial characteristics mediating the stress response: An exploratory study. *Personnel & Guidance Journal, 62,* 73–77.

Zygouris-Coe, V., Wiggins, M. B., & Smith, L. H. (2004). Engaging students with text: The 3-2-1 strategy. *The Reading Teacher, 58,* 381–384.

Index

CORWIN PRESS

The Corwin Press logo—a raven striding across an open book—represents the union of courage and learning. Corwin Press is committed to improving education for all learners by publishing books and other professional development resources for those serving the field of PreK–12 education. By providing practical, hands-on materials, Corwin Press continues to carry out the promise of its motto: **"Helping Educators Do Their Work Better."**